# Skills & Assignments in Communication Studies

An eight-page Tutor's Supplement is available to tutors from the publishers on request.

# Skills & Assignments in Communication Studies

## FOR BTEC NATIONAL LEVEL COURSES

### J Tuson
Formerly Head of English,
Clarendon College, Nottingham

and

### A T Jones
Senior Lecturer in English,
Chester College of Further Education

Stanley Thornes (Publishers) Ltd.

ISBN  0  85950  455  7


First published in 1979 by Stanley Thornes (Publishers) Ltd, Old Station Drive, Leckhampton, Cheltenham, GL53 0DN.


Reprinted 1983
Reprinted 1984 with corrections

Text in Stymie and Souvenir by Factel Ltd; Printed and bound in Great Britain at The Pitman Press, Bath.

# *Contents*

# Preface

The assignments in this book need not be approached chronologically, nor need all of them be completed, in order for the National Specifications to be fulfilled. The first two assignments are more straightforwad than the rest, however, and contain tasks which bridge 'O' level and BTEC work; while the last assignment will be most productive if left until the group know each other fairly well.

The check-lists on letter writing and report writing contain exercises and are, purposely, more thorough than the other check-lists since it is felt that students might prefer to develop these two crucial forms, separately, before being plunged into a full-scale assignment. The other check-lists, while acting as reminders of the accepted layout or common problems associated with any one form of communication, presume a fair amount of discussion by the class and direction by the tutor before they may be applied to specific tasks.

# Letter Writing

The ability to write effective letters is one of the most valuable business skills you can have. Although the telephone is being used more and more for short messages, it is an expensive means of communication and it may not even save you time, unless you can guarantee that the person you are ringing never leaves his office, and never says more than is strictly necessary, once you get through to him. Furthermore, when you send a letter you can keep a copy to check on the details and the person you are writing to can take as much time as he needs to consider your communication. Thus, communicating by letter has advantages for the person who sends the letter and its recipient (the person who receives it).

In this section, you are given advice about letter writing but very few hard-and-fast rules since each letter you write may demand a slightly different approach. The examples in this section demonstrate some of the factors which hinder clear and appropriate letter-writing but no-one can teach you how to build up a good relationship with your correspondents and even the lay-out of a letter is partly a matter of fashion or convenience and changes as occasion demands. The exercises in this section present you with a variety of problems so that you learn to be alert and flexible in dealing with correspondence, as well as being knowledgeable about accepted practice.

## THE LAYOUT OF THE LETTER

Letters to friends need to be clear and appropriate but their layout will be different from that used for business letters. In a business letter, the recipient's address (often called the 'inside address') should appear on the left hand side of the sheet and a reference, which normally comprises the initials of the person who composed the letter and those of the typist, is placed above it. The salutation, 'Dear Sir', may well be used and the correct complimentary close for this rather formal opening is, 'Yours faithfully' ('Yours sincerely', being the correct close only when the name of the recipient has appeared in the salutation.) The subject head (or heading) which sums up the purpose of the letter is another feature of business correspondence but it should only be used where the letter is of a fairly routine nature.

In a company, there may well be a standard 'house style' for laying out letters. Two common models are shown on pages 2 and 3; but many firms may use a mixture of the two. (You'll find examples of such 'hybrids' within this book, in fact.) These two model letters are written on paper which has the company's name and address (the 'letterhead') already printed. In this case, it is centred at the top of the sheet; but it could be in various other positions. A company's 'house style' may sometimes be designed to fit in with the printed letterhead; however, here both our common model layouts can be used successfully, as you will see.

# The 'Blocked' Layout

Notice the lack of indentation even for new paragraphs (extra space is left instead); the absence of punctuation above or below the body of the letter; and the limited use of commas within the body of the letter. This layout is becoming increasingly popular in business; because it is quicker to type, it is regarded as more efficient. (If the lack of commas in the body of the letter is overdone, however, it may not be so 'efficient' for someone trying to make sense of it!)

---

# AZ Assurance Limited

Prospect House   14-20 Main Road

Tellington TL3 6NJ

JMC/VS

3rd March 19–

The Sales Manager
Office Equipment Ltd
Enterprise Estate
Tellington Goodshire
TL3 6NT

Dear Sir

Flooring Estimate

Would you please arrange for a representative from your Flooring Department to visit our offices (at the address given above) before the end of March.

Our present floor covering is becoming worn and we would like estimates for both lino tiles and carpet squares.

I am dealing with this matter personally and can normally set aside some time in the afternoon to see your representative. If there are any difficulties over the timing, you can contact me by ringing Tellington 47615 Ext. 24.

Yours faithfully

J M Charles
Personnel Manager

---

# The 'Traditional' Layout

Note the more usual 'closed' punctuation and the position of the references, opposite the date which is always written in full.

---

# AZ Assurance Limited

Prospect House, 14-20 Main Road

Tellington TL3 6NJ

JMC/VS                                                    3rd March, 19—

The Sales Manager,
Office Equipment Ltd.,
Enterprise Estate,
Tellington, Goodshire.
TL3 6NT

Dear Sir,

Flooring Estimate

Would you please arrange for a representative from your Flooring Department to visit our offices (at the address given above) before the end of March.

Our present floor covering is becoming worn and we would like estimates for both lino tiles and carpet squares.

I am dealing with this matter personally, and can normally set aside some time in the afternoon to see your representative. If there are any difficulties over the timing, you can contact me by ringing Tellington 47615, Ext. 24.

Yours faithfully,

J M Charles
Personnel Manager

---

# Where there is no Printed Letterhead

Small organisations and individuals, of course, may not have pre-printed letterhead paper. In that case, using the 'blocked' layout would result in a confusing string of names and addresses down the left hand side. It may, therefore, be sensible to use the 'traditional' layout, which clearly separates the sender's and recipient's addresses. In the following example, only the recipient's address remains blocked. (This example is typed, but the same layout would work well for a handwritten letter. If you are writing as an individual, there is no need to put your name as well as the sender's address at the top. However, unless your signature is unusually clear, it is a good idea to print your name underneath it at the end of the letter.)

---

                                        Newtown Pigeon-Fanciers' Club,
                                        c/o 23 Farmington Road,
                                        Newtown.
                                        AS6 9BJ

Ref. 023/RMS                            14 May, 19—

The Sales Manager,
Portapigeon p.l.c.,
Nelson House,
65 Columbus Road,
Milchester.
MI13 0AB


Dear Sir,

                    Portapigeon Baskets Model 623

  Please send details of this new model, which you are advertising in
the latest issue of The Racing Pigeon. I believe it will be of considerable
interest to our members.

  I would be grateful if you could send, at the same time, a copy of your
complete catalogue.

            Yours faithfully,



            R.M. Smith
            Hon. Secretary

---

Standardisation of letter headings is not practised just to please examiners. Some organisations file by subject so a subject heading can be very helpful; others file by name so that the correct positioning of the reference may save a lot of delving into filing drawers; most importantly, all business organisations prefer to receive letters which are well written and clearly laid out. The habitual use of a helpful layout increases the efficiency of both the sender and the recipient and helps to create a good impression for the firm the letter represents.

It may be useful to set out the 'traditional' layout in diagramatic form. (This version assumes there is no printed letterhead.)

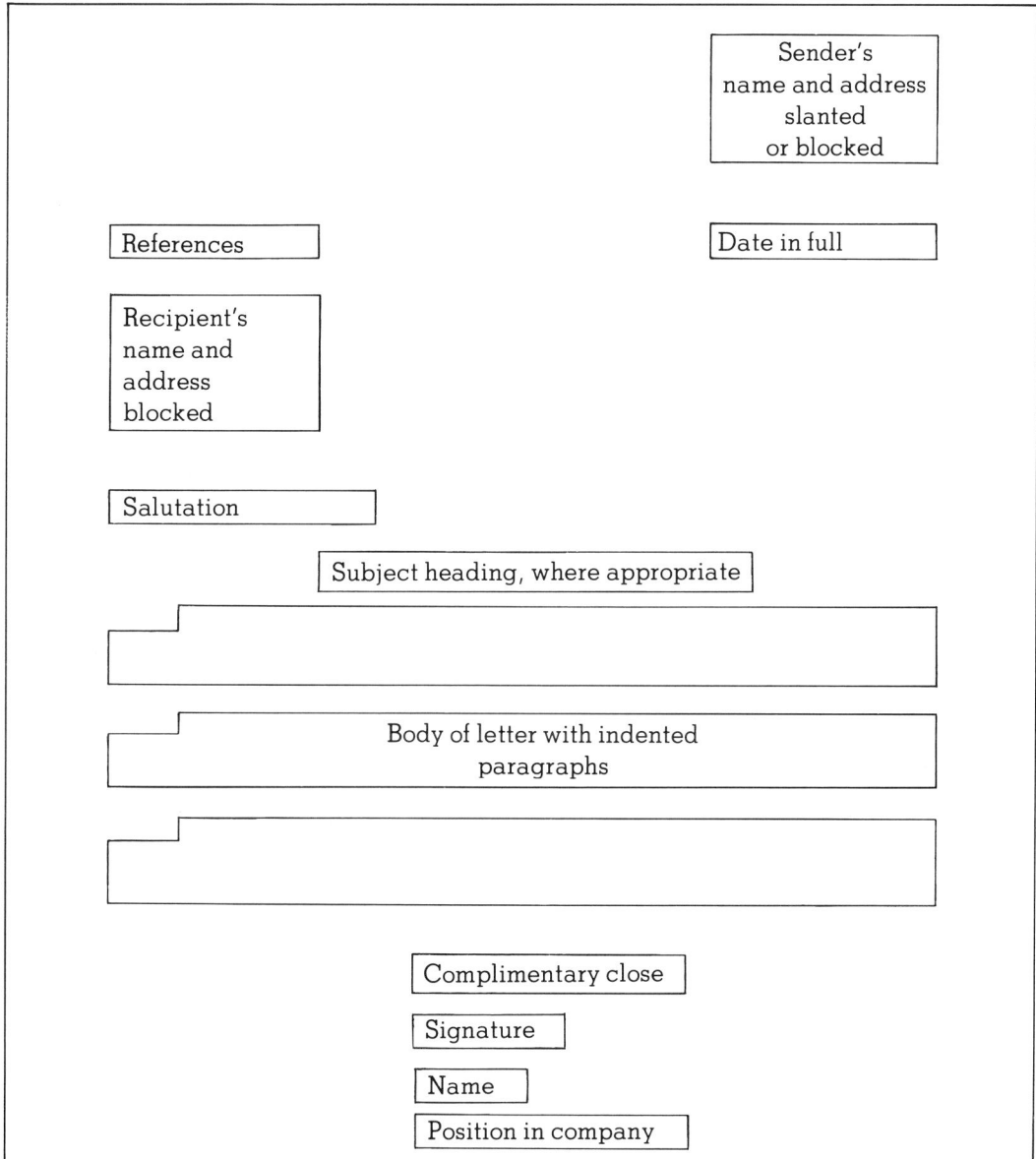

| | Sender's name and address slanted or blocked |

| References | | Date in full |

Recipient's
name and
address
blocked

Salutation

Subject heading, where appropriate

Body of letter with indented
paragraphs

Complimentary close

Signature

Name

Position in company

# THE BODY OF THE LETTER

Many business letters are so routine that, provided the layout is correct and the body of the letter is broken down into any necessary paragraphs, there can be little confusion. It is the complex or unusual letter which presents problems.

There are three main aspects to consider when composing the body of a letter:

1. the person sending the message,
2. the message being sent,
3. the person receiving the message.

These considerations overlap and interfuse but each one is important; as separating them reveals:

## The Sender

When writing any letter, the sender must know whether he is writing as an individual, giving his personal opinions, or whether he is representing his employer. You may have to compose letters for the signature of a superior where you disagree with both the content and style; but even if you are signing the business letters which you send out, you must avoid committing yourself to anything which does not have the backing of your employer. (cf. page 21 on Collection Letters). This type of diplomacy does not necessitate a cold, impersonal style, it merely requires you to recognise what is appropriate.

### Exercises

1. Write two letters to the local newspaper complaining about street traders: one from a local housewife and another from the Chairman of the local Chamber of Commerce.

2. Mr Rolf Vance, the new Director of your firm, believes in equality and so eats in the canteen with the workers instead of joining the other Directors in their private dining-room. Write a letter, as a co-Director warning Mr Vance that his action might be seen as 'snooping' by the work force. Write a letter, as the Trade Union Representative saying the same thing.

## The Message

The difficulty here is putting the message across as clearly and appropriately as possible. Problems with the message are avoided by good organisation and careful expression.

### Organisation of the Message

Failure to organise one's thoughts before beginning on a letter can result in a lack of clarity. The documents given below demonstrate the necessity of getting your facts right and adopting a plan before you even put pen to paper. The first document is the original telephone memo' which the Assistant Sales Manager used to compose a letter of apology to Mrs F Bradshaw and the second document is the confused and confusing letter that he eventually sent out.

---

# Fabrics by Post Ltd

**Downs Estate**
**Micklesham**
**3MK 4LA**

9th September 19—

Mrs F Broadshaw
8 The Grange
Micklesham
Mickleshire

Dear Mrs Broadshaw                                                        1

    With regard to the thirty metres of net curtaining. Presumably, you have now received your correct order and have sent the faulty material back to the supplier, enclosing the pre-paid envelope. If not

---

please let us know. As you are one of our oldest customers, I was very                    5
sorry you had been inconvenienced in this way and we hope you will
accept our sincere apologies.

When you rang unfortunately I was in a sales meeting with Mr
Clarke and could not deal with the phone-call but I have gone into the
matter most thoroughly since and I can assure you that this kind of        10
thing rarely happens here and that you need have no fear that it will
happen again and I hope that the enclosed voucher will convince you
of this and make up for your trouble.

Once again with my deepest apologies,

Yours sincerely                                                            15



Mr J Thwaite
Assistant Sales Manager

---

Even ignoring the rather brusque tone, the faults in this letter are numerous:

1. The first 'sentence' has no main verb. It also makes too vague a reference to the cause for complaint and is therefore confusing.
2. The opening paragraph dodges from "I" to "We" and changes subject on line 5. In general, the sentence and paragraph division is unhelpful.
3. Mr Thwaite has actually misread his instructions about the return of the nets (see line 3-5), and his request, "If not please let us know", is so indefinite that it is not clear which of the three separate parts to the question, Mrs B is expected to answer.
4. By pushing two separate points together on lines 5-7, Mrs B is given the impression that only certain customers are treated with respect and that she is considered geriatric.
5. The lack of punctuation on line 8 makes it unclear whether the call was unfortunate, or the sales meeting or Mr T's absence and this 'sentence' goes on for six lines.
6. The details of his whereabouts are unnecessary.
7. The vague, "this" on line 10 and "it", on line 11 causes confusion. Does "this" refer to his absence, slip-ups in despatch, or laddered net?
8. The information about the voucher is just tacked on the end of the explanation.
9. There is ambiguity surrounding the word "enclosed voucher" and Mrs B's "trouble".
10. The whole letter has no order to it. An obvious progress would have been a chronological one with a reference to the initial complaint, how it was investigated, what was done to correct the fault and what they promise to do in the future.

Several general rules can be made on the basis of these criticisms:

1. Try and use clear simple sentences and avoid figurative or ambiguous expression. (If you do not know what 'figurative' and 'ambiguous' mean – now is the time to find out!)
2. Make a definite reference to the reason for the letter and avoid the vague use of "this" or "it".
3. Get your facts straight and double-check any details of time or place.
4. Avoid repetition and lengthy explanation.
5. Develop your points by means of new sentences and paragraphs. Conciseness does not mean forcibly yoking ideas together.
6. Have a progress plan for the letter. Group associated points together and omit unnecessary detail.

## Exercises

1. Compose a suitable letter as instructed in the following memo paying particular attention to accuracy.

---

### Memorandum

**To:**  John Forbes                  **Date:**  4th December

**From:**  Alan White               **Subject:**  Section Lunch

I am attaching two lunch-time menus from nearby restaurants – bearing our £4 limit in mind, can you choose one and book us in for the 19th – there will only be 10 clerks since Mrs Thomas won't enter licensed premises on any account, but you will need to add you, me and our respective secretaries. (Ask them to confirm the booking in writing will you.)

---

# THE CHESTNUTS

All prices cover service and VAT

| | |
|---|---|
| Fruit Juice | 40p |
| Soup | 40p |
| Paté | 60p |

-oOo-

| | |
|---|---|
| Beef Stroganoff | £3.00 |
| Cod Portuguese | £3.00 |
| Lamb Navarin | £3.00 |
| Steak and Kidney Pie | £3.00 |
| Pork Epicée | £3.00 |
| Chicken Marengo | £3.00 |

Selected Vegetables Included

-oOo-

Sweet trolley from 60p – £1.00

## SPECIAL

Christmas Lunch (Dec 1st-31st)
Any starter and any sweet
with turkey and the trimmings
£3.50

Pid. 4291

# WINDHOVERS

Pid. 6481

Choice of Lunchtime Menus

at £3.20

Fruit Juice
Soup
Pate

-oOo-

Roast Beef
Roast Chicken
Roast Lamb
Pork or Veal Escalope

all with vegetables

-oOo-

Cheese and Biscuits
Ices
Fruit pie and custard

Service and VAT extra

2. The following letter is almost incomprehensible because of repetition and poor organisation. Rewrite it as simply and clearly as possible.

# Green Fingers Gardens Ltd

Shepley Road

Shepley

Ninshire

14th November, 19—

Mr V Jones,
Hardacres,
Wisley Fullerton,
Ninshire.


Dear Mr Jones,

We wish to acknowledge receipt of your order, which we received on the 10th September, and thank you for the same. Unfortunately, Mr Smith who usually deals with orders has now left the firm in order to retire but, as a new customer, you will be pleased to learn you are in line to qualify for our Lucky First Time Buyer Discount which is extended to all new customers during the winter months.

I am enclosing a catalogue with this letter as you requested but I am unable to send the special "Greenfingers Mini Tree" in red or white as yet, which was your initial reason for contacting us in the first place, since the public response has been so great. We are making every effort to rectify this situation as soon as possible but if we may venture some small piece of advice, we would suggest that you might be as well accepting the slightly smaller Dinky Tree, especially in view of the fact that it is just as sturdy in all weathers as the Mini Tree, and that we do have it in red and white whereas we only have the Mini Tree in yellow.

The First Time Buyer Discount is 20% provided you make your order before February but provided you make your order before, you do not have to accept delivery of it until growing conditions are suitable – both the Dinky and the Mini can go in at any time.

Once again we thank you for your esteemed order and assure you of our best services at all times.

Yours sincerely,


Mr A Fidd

## Expression of the message

While you might expect difficulties in communicating a message made up of complex ideas and information, you should note that the commonest of individual words, if it is mis-spelt or misused, can undermine your letter's efficiency. At this stage in your business career it is presumed that your spelling is fairly accurate and that you use a dictionary to look up unusual words. Even so there may be words about which you have a 'block'; often quite easy words that you have been mis-spelling for years, without realising it. Your spelling will normally be corrected when your work is marked, so one way to find out which are your 'blocks' and rid yourself of them is to look up any words which have been underlined in work that is returned to you.

Conscientious checking of this kind will also reveal the words you misuse. Words which sound similar or appear to be interchangeable when they are not, cause the most confusion. If a secretary wrote to complain about the draft, she would not thank you for closing all the windows since this is an example of a word which may be spelt in two different ways to give two different meanings. Confusion may also be caused where a word is only used in very specific contexts. Thus while you may go on an education course in order to be educated it is hoped that you will not be induced when you go on an induction course! (The verb is traditionally restricted to medical contexts even though the two words have the same stem.)

The emotional overtones attached to words may also restrict their use. You can say "Miss Muffat spoke softly, quietly or dulcetly" and all three are acceptable but to refer to a cushion as "quiet" or "dulcet" sounds foolish – in the case of the cushion, "soft" and "quiet" are not interchangeable because, while "soft" can be used to describe a wide number of materials or sensations, "quiet" is restricted to the description of sound. "Dulcet" is even more limited in its use, because it usually describes voices, mostly feminine ones and it always carries an emotional overtone suggesting beauty or charm. Thus the phrase "the dulcet grunt of a sow" could only be used sarcastically even though it obeys the restrictions of sound and femininity. There is no easy way of teaching this kind of 'emotional' distinction between words. A wide vacabulary can only be obtained by a lot of intelligent reading and listening. Thus, unless you have a dictionary handy, a general rule with regard to vocabulary in business correspondence is that you should only include those words which you are *sure* you spell and use correctly.

**Exercises**

1. To help you check if you are confusing words which sound similar or seem to be related, go through the list, given below, placing each word into a sentence which clearly shows its meaning. (This list contains words whose use is almost unavoidable in business letters.)

| | | | |
|---|---|---|---|
| affect | effect | dependent | dependant |
| enquire | inquire | respectfully | respectively |
| draft | draught | uninterested | disinterested |
| alternate | alternative | weather | whether |

2. To ensure that you appreciate the different overtones associated with words,

look at the sentences below and explain why the italicised words in each series are being used incorrectly.

(a)   (i) I have received your swift reply.
       (ii) I have received your *hurried* reply.
       (iii) I have received your *brisk* reply.

(b)   (i) Did you build that wall?
       (ii) Did you *make* that wall?
       (iii) Did you *create* that wall?

(c)   (i) He certainly kept a clear head.
       (ii) He certainly kept an *empty* head.
       (iii) He certainly kept a *transparent* head.

# The Recipient

Obviously, the words chosen to express a message will partly depend upon the nature of that message. A letter of complaint will use very different language from a letter of friendly enquiry, for example. Consideration of the person who will receive the message will also affect your choice of language, however, and, in some cases, the status of the recipient will override the tone suggested by the nature of the message.

In the central heating letters, which follow, Mrs Tilney is employing Mr Brownslow so she feels able to cajole or criticise him as the occasion demands, but if Mrs Tilney had cause to complain to the local Bishop about the poor standard of organ-playing in the diocese, she might not be so brusque.

Although Mrs Tilney's letters are both to the same person, they are tailored to suit the recipient, in one sense, because she presumes that Mr Brownslow, like most people, prefers praise to criticism. In the first letter, she hopes to flatter him into granting her request: in the second, she hopes to frighten him into removing her cause for complaint. Mrs Tilney may have misjudged her recipient on both occasions but it is important to note how the letter changes once Mr Brownslow is no longer 'the friend' but has become 'the enemy'

# Request to a Friend

Greenways,
The Paddock,
Miln,
Fromshire.

Mr J Brownslow,                            14th December, 19—
Hotspot Ltd.,
Jesford, Fromshire,
JS4 2FL

Dear Mr Brownslow,

    Thank you for your speedy reply to my request for an estimate. I would like you to begin installation as soon as possible.

Your heating engineers came to the house yesterday and after inspecting the plumbing, were able to assure me that extension of the existing central heating system should present no problems.

I was so impressed by this efficiency that I am tempted to ask a favour. Would it be possible for them to have the new radiators installed before the holiday? I realise that you have other orders to attend to but I would be grateful if you could "squeeze me in" somewhere since we are having guests to stay over Christmas and it would be nice to give them a really warm welcome!

Yours sincerely,

Mrs F Tilney

## Complaint to an 'Enemy'

Greenways,
The Paddock,
Miln,
Fromshire.

18th December, 19—

Hotspot Ltd.,
Jesford, Fromshire,
JS4 2FL

Dear Sir,

I am disgusted! The workmen rolled up on Wednesday; both of them totally incompetent and more than a little inebriated. Having fiddled around with the boiler for two hours, they mumbled something about water pressure, and left without restoring the hot water, and without any indication as to when they might return.

The official estimate promised completion within three days of work commencing and I certainly intend to hold you to this agreement. I should prefer you to send trained staff this time but if the original pair must return, I would be grateful if they would moderate their drinking and their language.

Failing the completion of the work within the agreed period, my husband has decided to seek redress at the local Department of Fair Trading.

Yours faithfully,


Mrs F Tilney

Tailoring a letter to its recipient starts at the most basic level of layout. 'Dear Sir' or 'Dear Madam' could be seen as suitably polite or offensively impersonal depending on the relationship which exists between the person sending the letter and the recipient. Certainly, many business concerns now address the recipient by name wherever possible, unless they actively wish to project a formal tone. Similarly, a subject heading may make a letter seem too brisk if one has a personal relationship with the recipient and the original rule of conciseness may have to be waived in favour of a more leisurely, friendly presentation.

Consideration of the recipient will also affect the body of the letter. If your recipient is in the same line of business as yourself, he may well share your technical jargon (although he may resent its use in a letter). With a member of the public, however, painstaking explanation may be necessary and even common business jargon will cause confusion ("your letter of the 15th ult" will mean *nothing* to the vast majority of the population who do not work in offices).

In the same way, while a tone of friendly banter might be acceptable in a letter to a colleague; a member of the public may regard such a tone as disrespectful or sarcastic, and the tone of detached correctness necessary to some official letters will be seen as officious and brusque if used in everyday correspondence. In general, a tone of helpful efficiency will be correct but where a more specific tone is necessary, the nature of the relationship between the sender and the recipient coupled with the nature of the message will provide your guide lines.

The tone of any letter depends upon several factors, the most important of these being:

1. the vocabulary,
2. the form of the verb,
3. and the punctuation.

# Vocabulary

On page 12 you saw how words with similar meanings were not interchangeable if they had different emotional overtones. When you are trying to project and maintain a certain tone, it is the 'emotional' element in the vocabulary which you must consider. In Mrs Tilney's letters on central heating (pages 13/15) the professional-sounding, "engineers" have turned into "workmen", once they have bungled the job and their, "inspection of the plumbing" contrasts strongly with her later description of the way they "fiddled around with the boiler".

Interestingly, although vocabulary or expressions which are close to slang (like, "fiddled around") always lower the tone of a letter, they can suggest friendliness or aggression, depending on the context. Mrs Tilney's use of, "squeeze me in", is deliberately coy and chatty: the phrase implies that she and Mr Brownslow are equals. Her use of, "rolled up" and, "fiddled around" however, is insulting: the informality of the expressions signifying the low esteem which she has for the workmen's abilities.

In the same way, technical or genteel words usually raise the tone of a letter and may lend dignity to the person writing the letter and to the letter's content. Thus, Mrs Tilney's, "failing completion" and, "seeks redress" emphasise her seriousness and make the letter formal and legal-sounding. If this high tone is used unnecessarily, however, either to communicate a trivial message or when more straightforward vocabulary could be used, the tone of the letter might become pompous, sarcastic or even unintentionally funny.

## The Form of the Verb

The difference in tone obtained by using the first person or third person can easily be demonstrated:

"I would like to thank you for your concern" (first person) is more friendly than, "The manager would like to thank you for your concern" (third person) and making the verb impersonal, with no reference to 'I' or 'we', makes the letter positively cold: "Your concern has been received with thanks". Thus, in the second central heating letter (page 14), the first person, "I am disgusted" stresses the immediacy of Mrs Tilney's anger but the stern, third person decision to, "seek redress at the local Office of Fair Trading" is much more threatening.

The tense of the verb also affects tone. Using the present tense will always make the tone more immediate. (Mr Tilney's, "I am disgusted" is like a slap in the face.) The conditional tense, however, may make the tone polite or sarcastic, depending on the context. Thus the words, "I would be most grateful", which are used in both central heating letters, are meant to be taken as a gracious plea in the first letter and as a rebuke in the letter of complaint. (Note also the use of the imperative (an order) when you want the message to sound urgent.)

## Punctuation

Your use of punctuation will also affect the tone of a letter. Generally, short sentences suggest strong emotion and keep the recipient on his toes, while longer sentences allow him to relax. As the exception which proves the rule, Mrs Tilney's sentence beginning, "Having fiddled", is fairly long and yet it gives little comfort to Mr Brownslow. In this case, the angry tone has been maintained by the list-like punctuation which serves to reinforce the tedious nature of the workmen's mistakes and her own exasperation.

Note also, the effect of rhetorical questions!
"You know about it do you?"

"You don't know about it do you?"
"You know about it don't you?"
"Surely you know about it don't you?" etc.

Unless vocabulary, verbs and punctuation are used subtly and together, the tone of a letter can become totally inconsistent; with both a lack of clarity and an inappropriateness, which confounds the message. The ability to decide on the correct tone and maintain it is the most difficult of the letter writing skills and it may need to be practised long after considerations of layout and organisation present no problem.

**Exercises**   In the following letters the tone is both inappropriate and uneven. Re-write them so that the tone is suitable and the message is clear – being particularly careful to assess the nature of the message in the light of the recipient.

---

# Grumble & Shark
Oxford Street
London

Cosmetics Consultant,                                               17 August, 19—
Toiletries Section,
Birmingham Store.

Dear Employee,

### Staff Changes

It has come to the notice of management that the sales figures for cosmetics in the store, where you have your job, are not keeping pace with those experienced by other sales staff in our provincial branches.

As an old employee of Grumble & Shark, you cannot fail to have noticed that a more colourful and trendy type of customer now frequents the Birmingham store and it is felt that this may, in part, explain your lack of success with regard to improving turnover.

After consultation, management has decided to move you from cosmetics to garden tools where it is felt that you would be more usefully employed.

Yours faithfully,

T. Purser
pp Julius Grumble Junior

---

# BUILDABOAT
## Tel. 0231-6741 Telex. 58612
### "Over 100 boats assembled on show at our Freeston Lock Marina"

Buildaboat
Freeston Lock
Fromshire

23rd April, 19—

Mr P N Rogers
'Westward Ho'
Piddlington, Wessex

Dear Mr Rogers,

<u>Boat trailer prototype</u>

We are in receipt of your letter of the 8th inst. in which you offer us the marketing rights for your boat trailer, and our PR man is longing to meet you.

We understand that you have also contacted Bettaboats Ltd but I don't think they have our dynamism. As you know, though a young firm, we are really making it big with self-build lines and while boat-trailers are not really our scene, this one is something else. We are always on the look out for a design which will catch the public eye and which is economically viable, viz prevailing market trends.

We realise that travelling presents a problem for retired people such as your good self and we also have every sympathy for your request for anonymity since, when in production, your idea could well make you filthy rich. Thus our PR man intends visiting you personally, Thursday of next week if that is O.K. by you? Give us a ring if it is inconvenient.

Yours sincerely,

Barry Gibbs
(Managing Director)

# Additional Exercises in Letter Writing

1. Compose a letter from the Manager of Hotel Excellence, to Lady Foxley-Smyth explaining that the suite overlooking Trafalgar Square which she normally occupies for the month of February, will not be available until the 12th of that month, since the entire hotel has been booked by an Arab oil Sheikh and his entourage for a six week period to coincide with the January Sales.

2. Compose a letter to the local newspaper applauding or condemning a recent decision by the County Leisure Services to ban smoking in the town's community centre (which also houses a bar, a restaurant, and the only sport hall and cinema in the area).

3. Write a letter to your boss explaining your 'extraordinary behaviour' at the office party.

4. Compose a reply to a laundry servicing enquiry from Scientific Supplies Ltd., Downs Estate, Plowsville, paying particular attention to the ordering of information and avoiding unnecessary detail. Use the following price lists and advertising literature as the basis for your letter.

---

## EAST-WEST LAUNDRY SERVICES
20-30 London Road, Plowsville
Domestic — Hotel — Commercial — Industrial

**Price List**

Sheets 30p per item 25% discount on 20 or more per week. Pillow-cases and small table cloths 10p per item 25% discount, as above. Large table-cloths and bedspreads 50p — £2 depending on size and material.
Starching 10p extra per item (any size)
Sheets 15p per item £1 per ten.

Entire individual laundry £2 per week £80 per annum.
Entire family laundry (4 persons ) £6 per week £250 per annum.
Individual towels 10p per item, 25% discount on 20 or more per week.
Roller towels 15p per item and installation charge.
Boiler suits/overalls/laboratory coats 20p per item 25% discount as above.

---

## EAST-WEST — ALWAYS BEST
### HOTEL AND COMMERCE PACKAGE

If you have more than 30 items laundered per week, you may be entitled to our:

### 30% BULK DISCOUNT OFFER
Contact: The Sales Manager,
East-West, 20-30 London Road., Plowsville
Tele: 621907

5. In letter writing exercises, you may have to use your imagination in order to complete the instructions to the full. Some people find this difficult, but at least no one can challenge the 'facts' you produce in this way and the structure of the letter will usually be defined by the wording of the question. In the business setting, the information which you need in order to produce an efficient letter may not always be to hand. The most appropriate tone for use with a particular recipient may have to be deduced from brief phone calls or earlier correspondence and several documents may have to be taken into account before you can give an adequate reply to an enquiry. The document-based papers in the second half of this book will help you to practise this process of collection and collation by requiring you to search out information from several sources just as you do at work; but you might begin with the one fairly demanding document given below:

List the points of information which will have to be included in a reply to the letter from Mr Green and indicate the clues to his character and status which may have to be taken into account when deciding on an appropriate tone for the letter.

6, New Street,
WEDLEY.

14 April 1979

Dear Sir,

I am writting to tell you about the meater. We share it with Flat 4 bevor they leave I do not no were they went. We did not stealled it I bet the stealled it they were a bad lot. ALL the money was gone so we can not pay I say tell the polis but may be they put us away if we do We do not go the

the door if people came in case of polis. If you come you must tell us when you come and what you cloths you have.

You got to help we got no electric and we stay indoor so they can not find us. You wont tell the polis if the polis come Mrs Green say to kill her She is porly and prison will kill her. The PENSION book is all my mony I put it in the on velob so that you no we are not theve. You must take the money out for us.

MR GREEN

This letter is not a joke – according to one estimate there are as many as 6 million semi-literates in Britain.

# Ten Points to Note

1. *Applications.* You should begin by naming the post for which you are applying and stating where you saw it advertised. (Large firms may have advertised several posts in several newspapers so accuracy on your part can save confusion and help the firm decide which advertisement was the most effective.) Points to include are: educational and professional qualifications, previous experience, why you want the particular post, the names and addresses of referees, relevant domestic details and pertinent general skills (eg a clean driving licence). The letter of application will normally be handwritten but where supporting details are numerous they may be typed on a separate sheet.

2. *Circulars.* The salutation should be suitably wide, eg 'Dear Colleagues' or 'Dear Customers'. If the circular is an advertisement the first sentences should attract the recipient's attention. If it is for wide circulation, it is not necessary to include the date.

3. *Collection Letter or Complaints.* This type of letter should not be sent until an explanation has been requested. You may be mistaken and so cause unnecessary ill-feeling by acting hastily. You must not threaten action unless you can carry it out, abuse anyone or make accusations which you cannot prove.

4. *House Style.* If your employer prefers one particular layout and style of letter and uses it, then you must too. The underlying principles of clarity and appropriateness remain the same and you can always adopt a less idiosyncratic form for examination purposes.

5. *Invitations.* Formal invitations are usually printed and are in the third person (eg The Directors of Hawkins Ltd request the pleasure . . . etc). Whether formal or informal the details must be double-checked.

6. *Postal Code.* The postal code should preferably be on a separate line with a space between the two halves. The characters should not be joined and neither punctuation nor underlining should be used.

7. *Reply to Complaints.* It is not necessary to keep repeating your apologies. An apology and an explanation are sufficient.

8. *Signatures.* If the letter has been written in the first person ('I') it will normally conclude with the writer's signature followed by the post he holds. Where the person who composed the letter is a fairly junior member of staff, however, he might sign his name but follow the signature with the abbreviation pp (on behalf of) and then the name of his senior or the firm. The name of the firm on its own is only suitable for the most routine letters.

9. *Titles.* 'Esquire' is preferable to 'Mr' if the recepient has letters after his name. 'Mr' and 'Esq' however, should never be used together, and you must know the initials of the recipient if you wish to use Esq. after his name. (eg I G Write Esq). The correct way to address titled recipients will be found in 'Titles and Forms of Address', published by Adam and Charles Black

10 *Window Envelopes.* If a window envelope is used it is more convenient to place the inside address at the bottom of the letter so that it may be easily folded to fit 'the window'.

# Report Writing

Report writing is a task which causes unnecessary problems to many students. It is often regarded by employers as the supreme test of a young executive's competence, hence the number of Report Writing courses demanded by industry and offered by colleges all over the country.

From the employee's point of view, report writing is particularly trying because the end product is always intended for the eyes of his bosses, a disadvantage not shared by letters, which are normally free from the icy scrutiny of superiors.

It is a relief, therefore, to learn that there is a simple formula which, if followed, ensures that all reports are logical in their development and do not omit any necessary information. This formula is based upon the five traditional headings under which reports were written, namely:

1. Terms of Reference.
2. Proceedings.
3. Evidence.
4. Conclusions.
5. Recommendations.

Most reports at this level do not require the use of these five headings as such, simply because the reports are not long enough to justify a five part division, but the headings are nevertheless useful to us because they represent a series of questions which, if answered in order, will always produce a satisfactory report. The questions are as follows:

1. *Terms of Reference.* What is the report about and who commissioned it?
2. *Proceedings.* What steps did you take to discover your information?
3. *Evidence.* What information was obtained?
4. *Conclusions.* How would you sum up the main points of your evidence?
5. *Recommendations.* What action do you recommend?

Let us take a typical case by way of illustration – typical both in the real world of work and in professional examinations. You have been asked by your employer to report upon poor timekeeping in the office where you work.

# what is the report about and who commissioned it?

At the request of the General Manager I investigated complaints of poor timekeeping in the Accounts Office.

# what steps did you take to discover your information?

In order to ascertain the facts I interviewed the 16 employees in this section and checked their times of arrival each morning for a fortnight.

# what information was obtained?

Of the 16 employees, 12 relied upon public transport and four arrived by car. Those who arrived by car were generally punctual but those arriving by the 124 bus from the town centre were often as much as ten minutes late.

This bus should stop outside the office at 8.55 a.m. but my observations confirmed that it was very erratic in its time of arrival and that the passengers could not be blamed for bing late. An earlier bus arrived outside the office at 8.30 a.m.

# how would you sum up the main points of your evidence?

The staff cannot reasonably be expected to arrive 30 minutes early each day to avoid being a few minutes late occasionally, but changes in the office routine could diminish the problem.

# what action do you recommend?

I recommend that those staff who travel by public transport be given the option of starting work at 8.45 a.m. and finishing 15 minutes early. This would be advantageous to them in that the 8.30 bus would allow them to arrive in comfortable time for work even allowing for delays and would be advantageous to the office in that the working day would be slightly extended.

Now read the report again, this time ignoring the questions. You will see that it proceeds smoothly from point to point and that nothing is omitted. This point is further illustrated in the two versions of the same report printed below.

The first version leaves one with a general sense of what has happened but the actual details are confused and it is the reader who is left to give form and coherence to the material; in the second version the material is organised according to our five part plan and the development is clear and uncluttered.

# First Version

**To:**   Medical Officer of Health

**From:**   A Jones (Health Visitor)

Mrs R Dixon of 13 New Road, Newtown, finds it impossible to climb stairs or heat all the downstairs rooms, which is why she is living in the kitchen. This is aggravating the bronchial complaint of which Dr Pritchard informed us and the situation cannot but get worse if nothing is done. Mrs Dixon has been unable to climb stairs since the death of her husband 18 months ago and now sleeps on a camp bed in one corner of the kitchen. I was able to ascertain these facts during my weekly visits to New Road between November 10th and December 17th. During the coldest days even the kitchen is inadequately heated and the damp atmosphere of that room is hardly healthy for a bronchial sufferer. Perhaps alternative accommodation more suited to the needs of an elderly person could be found for Mrs Dixon as soon as possible. I know that Dr Pritchard shares my views on the unsuitability of her present situation.

# Second Version

**To:**   Medical Officer of Health

**From:**   A Jones (Health Visitor)

### Mrs R Dixon, 13 New Road, Newtown

Dr Pritchard informed us on 31st October that Mrs Dixon's health was deteriorating rapidly as a result of her unsatisfactory living conditions. She suffers particularly badly from bronchial complaints.

I visited New Road five times between November 10th and December 17th to get to know Mrs Dixon's problems for myself.

Since the death of her husband 18 months ago Mrs Dixon has been forced to live in one room of her house, as she cannot climb the stairs unaided and cannot afford to heat more than one of the downstairs rooms. She washes and cooks in the kitchen and also sleeps there on a camp bed. Even this one room is barely warm on the coldest days and the damp atmosphere is aggravating her bronchial complaint.

I agree with Dr Pritchard that Mrs Dixon's ill health is directly attributable to the conditions in which she lives and that the situation is getting worse.

I recommend that alternative accommodation more suited to the needs of an elderly person be found for Mrs Dixon as soon as possible.

# Headings in Reports

You will notice that a memo type layout and a heading are used in place of a sentence explaining the subject of the report in the second version. This is perfectly good practice and whether you use it will depend both upon your personal judgment and upon the report format demanded by the organisation for which you work.

We have already decided not to use the five traditional report headings outlined earlier, but there are advantages to the use of some of them in a modified form, especially where the report is becoming very complex or when it exceeds about four hundred words in length. The reader will be made aware at a glance of the order in which the information is to be conveyed to him and will be grateful to you for your consideration. Let us, therefore, consider which of the headings are useful and which are not.

## Terms of Reference

It would be somewhat pedantic to describe the simple instructions issued to most report writers in business as 'Terms of Reference'. It is also a technical term which would do nothing to clarify your aims to someone not certain of its meaning.

Do make certain, however, that you have been given precise instructions before you begin writing your report. Managers who complain about poor reports from their subordinates are often themselves to blame in that the instructions they issued in the first place were inadequate or unclear.

We shall not, therefore, be using the heading "Terms of Reference".

## Proceedings

The objections we made to Terms of Reference also apply here and this heading will not be used by us.

The headings, Terms of Reference and Proceedings, will be combined by us under the one heading 'Introduction'. Take care not to include any of your evidence in this section. Regard it purely as a reminder to your boss of the report's purpose and a statement of the steps taken by you in gathering information.

## Evidence

This is the heart of the report and the heading must obviously appear. It heralds the end of the introductory section and the start of the report proper. The evidence may itself be sub-divided into shorter sections, each with a numbered sub-heading.

## Conclusions

In a short report where recommendations are asked for it is not likely that the conclusions will assume sufficient importance to merit a section of their own. Indeed, in many brief reports a summary of the evidence may well appear superfluous. Do try to produce such a summary, however, brief though it may be, because your familiarity with the material in question will often lead you to regard as glaringly obvious points which to a reader unacquainted with the situation are anything but clear.

Where Recommendations are asked for, Conclusions are combined with Evidence, to produce one section bearing the latter heading.

## Recommendations

If recommendations are asked for they must be placed in a separate section under this heading. Multiple recommendations are best numbered and must be clearly expressed as courses of action which you recommend should be put into practice. A common error is to phrase them as further conclusions rather than specific recommendations.

Where recommendations are not asked for they must clearly not be made, however strong the temptation at times. In such a case the conclusions assume a much greater importance and are given a section of their own, because it is only through the conclusions that you can hope to influence the decisions that will be taken at a higher level. Take great care not to make specific recommendations, however, as this might well be regarded as an impertinence on your part.

In both cases we are left with three headings as follows.

Where recommendations *are* asked for:
1. Introduction.
2. Evidence.
3. Recommendations.

Where recommendations *are not* asked for:
1. Introduction.
2. Evidence.
3. Conclusions.

The completed report should be dated and signed. If the report has been produced by a group of people it is normally signed by the Chairman, the names of the other group members having been listed in the introduction.

A final check for grammatical errors and careless slips always pays dividends at this stage, and if you suspect that any part of the report is ambiguous it is wise to ask a third party, not connected with the writing of the report, to read it and give his opinion. You may then submit it with some degree of confidence to the scrutiny of your superiors.

A completed report, where recommendations are asked for, will now have the following layout:

```
┌─────────────────────────────────────────────────────────────────────┐
│                                                                       │
│          A Report on Poor Timekeeping in the Accounts Department      │
│                                                                       │
│       Introduction                                                    │
│                                                                       │
│       _____     │
│                                                                       │
│       _____     │
│                                                                       │
│                                                                       │
│       Evidence                                                        │
│                                                                       │
│       _____     │
│                                                                       │
│       _____     │
│                                                                       │
│       _____     │
│                                                                       │
│       _____     │
│                                                                       │
│       _____     │
│                                                                       │
│                                                                       │
│       Recommendations                                                 │
│                                                                       │
│           1. _____      │
│                                                                       │
│           _____     │
│                                                                       │
│           2. _____      │
│                                                                       │
│           _____     │
│                                                                       │
│                                                                       │
│       Date                      Signature                             │
│                                                                       │
│                                                                       │
└─────────────────────────────────────────────────────────────────────┘
```

As you gain more experience of report writing by working through the various assignments in this book you will begin to discover other ways in which your reports can be improved. For instance, it is often possible to divide your evidence into numbered sections and so to frame your recommendations that they deal with the same numbered points in the same order. If you are asked to produce a lengthy report you may find it useful to intersperse your evidence with conclusions as you proceed, before bringing all these conclusions together at the end of the section.

Whatever else you do, think always of your reader, adapt your writing style to his needs and use any devices of layout or classification which will make his task easier.

Should you forget all else, remember the oldest communications rule of them all:

"First tell your reader what you are going to tell him, (Introduction) then tell him, (Evidence) then tell him what you have told him, (Conclusion)". You should work through a sample of the following exercises before proceeding to the full length assignments.

**Exercises**

1. Select one of the following aspects of college life and write a brief report on your classmates' attitudes towards it.

| | |
|---|---|
| The Canteen. | Decorative Condition of the Classrooms. |
| Sports Facilities. | Provision of Cycle and Motorcycle Sheds. |
| The Library. | Allocation of Lockers. |
| The Students' Union. | |

2. Conduct a survey of your classmates' attitudes towards any subject of general concern and write a brief report stating your conclusions clearly. Subjects of interest might include:

| | |
|---|---|
| Smoking and its Dangers. | Soccer Hooliganism. |
| Violence on Television. | Is Homework Necessary? |

3. A number of last year's school leavers have been asked to report to the County Careers Officer on the careers guidance they received at school. Write a report outlining your own experiences.

4. Question your mother or father about any item of equipment they use regularly in the home, eg an electric drill, a washing machine, and report as if to the manufacturers on their opinion as to its soundness for the job it is intended to perform.

5. Invite a lecturer from another department to talk briefly about the courses offered in his department. Question him on what other courses he thinks could be provided or how present courses could be improved, and write a report giving his recommendations.

6. Your college will hold a fire drill early during the first term. (If no drill is held take it up with the Students' Union.) Observe carefully what happens and write a report to the College Safety Committee making any recommendations you see fit for future improvements.

7. *For day release students only.* Write a report on the induction procedure you underwent when you joined your present employer. You are to recommend to the Personnel Officer any improvements suggested by your experience.

8. Unless you are very lucky, your college will have a car parking problem. Observe the situation and make any recommendations you can for its improvement. These will probably be welcomed by the Vice-principal who is often delegated this thankless task.

9. Interview one of the following College Officers on his or her responsibilities and write a report to the Students' Union Committee:

| | |
|---|---|
| a. Accommodation Officer. | d. Welfare Officer. |
| b. Safety Officer. | e. Careers Officer. |
| c. Tutor in Adult Literacy. | |

10. Examine your old school reports. How far did the layout allow the teachers to express clearly what they wanted to say? Were these reports generally fair? Write a report to your old headmaster making recommendations for improvements. (Note to tutors: School Reports are confidential documents, students should not be asked to bring them to college.)

## CHECK LIST FOR CHARTS AND NOTICES

There are two essential considerations in the writing of effective charts and notices. All necessary details must be included, but the appearance should remain uncluttered and appealing.

Use numbering, underlining, indentation, heavy type, etc. to help separate information and use shock headings etc. if you want to attract attention.

(Before designing a chart or notice, analyse several posters or advertisements and consider both their psychological appeal and their presentation.)

# A Problem for the Celtic Association

1. You are secretary of the local Celtic Association which is holding its Annual General Meeting on St. Patrick's Day in an upstairs room at 'The Bull' (Document A). Write a general notice of meeting, to be placed on notice-boards around the town and an open letter of invitation which may be sent out to members, in a duplicated form, as required.

2. A patriotic student-group has misunderstood your meeting and sees it as a rally in support of Home Rule for the Celts. They force entry, carrying banners and break up the meeting by heckling just before the end of the Finance Report. Having glanced at the verbatim report of the proceedings (Document B) write a letter to the press describing this infringement and asking for an apology in the strongest terms.

3 Mr McLintock, one of the older members, was cut by broken glass during the scuffling and was sent to the hospital suffering from shock. They decided to keep him there for observation. A well-meaning lady member sends you a letter (Document C) to forward to him on behalf of all the members. Whilst not wishing to change the sentiments or offend the lady, you decide that you will remove the ambiguities and other mistakes before sending it.

4. Your society has decided to try to claim damages from the student-group. Write a summary of the exchanges between members and students (Document B) in reported speech in order to present it to your solicitor.

Limit 200 words.

# Document A

Annual General Meeting of the Celtic Association in the upper rooms of 'The Bull' on St. Patrick's Day (March 17th) at 7.30 p.m.

## AGENDA

1. Apologies for absence.

2. Minutes of previous meeting.

3. Matters arising from minutes.

4. Correspondence.

5. Chairman's remarks.

6. Treasurer's report.

7. Motions.

   (a)  That no new applications for membership should be accepted from tee-totallers.

   (b)  That membership fees should be increased to cover the rising cost of heating, etc.

   Proposed: Mrs Davies.    Seconded: Miss Griffith.

8. Any other business.

---

# Document B

Verbatim Report by the Secretary

Exchanges between Members and Students at the Celtic Association Meeting.

**Treasurer:** So you see, although we are in the red at the moment, we should be able to remedy this situation once the profits from the first dance are included.

**Student:** Get back to Ireland mate – we don't want your kind here. Why don't you go back where you came from? You're not wanted here I tell you.

**Chairman:** Silence! Silence! Who told you you could come in here like this? What do you think you are doing? You can't just come in here like that.

**Student:** You come into England and take our jobs. Why don't you get back where you came from? We've got enough unemployed of our own.

**Chairman:** I think you must be mistaken, sir. Personally, I own my own business and I don't see that that is harming anybody.

**Girl Student:** We've got enough trouble in this country without you lot. Why don't you keep to your business and leave us to deal with our own trouble. We were born in this country and we like it the way it is – if you don't like it, get out – don't try messing with other people's business.

| Chairman: | My dear young lady, I really cannot think what this is all about, but I can assure you that the affairs of this meeting are of a very friendly nature and of local importance only. We are not a political concern – no indeed, we are merely a group of friends meeting for amusement. |
|---|---|
| Student: | We know your kind – you may be friendly now but who is to say that tomorrow you won't be wielding a machine-gun? |
| Chairman: | (amidst laughter) I don't think I would even know which end to hold one. |
| Girl Student: | You can laugh . . . you can laugh, but you can't stop us. We are going to break up your meeting and you can't stop us. Come on, patriots, get them. |

At this point several of the students moved forward and jostled those members standing at the bar. They defended themselves by pushing back but were unable to prevent two students from breaking tables and chairs. Others of them ripped down the green flag which hangs above the rostrum and during this manoeuvre the mirror at the back of the hall was dislodged and fell to the ground sending pieces of glass everywhere and, I think, cutting Mr McLintock who fell off the rostrum and lay in great terror on the floor while everything raged on around him. Finally there was a cry of 'Police' and the young people ran away, leaving us to face the angry publican who made us straighten the furniture and sweep the floor even though several people had cuts and bruises and were obviously suffering from shock.

# Document C

The Lady Member's Letter to Mr McLintock.

---

Dear Mr McLintock,

I am writing to say how sorry I am that you narrowly missed getting hurt the other day. I have seen other members and each wants to send their best wishes – try and forget all about it and you'll soon be in the pink.

You must not think you have been forgotten. Mr Macleod sat up all night worrying and caught a cold in his pyjamas. I always have said that as soon as you're down, they forget you and I am the last person to offend myself but I only found out about you the other day and then I decided to waste no time in writing.

Mary can't come and see you this week because grandma is poorly and you know how she is!

Best wishes for your recovery,


Mrs Jones

P.S.   I was told you were being converted . . . Shall I see the gas-man for you or would you prefer him to wait  When did you arrange to have him?

---

## CHECK LIST FOR DISCUSSIONS

Unless discussions are approached in a clear-headed way they can lead to misunderstandings and argument.

1. Listen carefully to other speakers and clarify any of their remarks which are confusing or open-ended by asking: "Do you mean that . . .?" or "Are you saying that . . .?"

2. Note any important points which you wish to support or deny later and also note any definite stages reached in the discussion.

3. Do not offer any information or opinion which you are not empowered to give.

4. Be alert to points which have not been cleared up and ask appropriate, specific questions so as to bring these into the open.

5. Before the group separates, summarise the discussion and obtain agreement on the position reached. (If a senior member of staff is present or a chairman, this job will fall to him.)

Practise  listening out for the tone in which ideas are put forward or the way in which a subject is broached.

Test your ability to frame appropriate questions by jotting down the information you would require to:

1. Arrange a trip to Edinburgh from London for a business conference on the second Thursday and Friday in May. (You will be travelling with two senior colleagues and expenses are limited.)

2. Book seats at a London Theatre, as a celebration for your BEC group when they pass their examination.

The check list, above, is for informal meetings. The best way of checking communications for formal meetings is to browse through several notices of agenda and minutes from different organisations. (The public library will have copies of local government committees and you could compare these with those of a student committee or of any club of which you are a member.)

As a rough guide, agendas should follow a similar order to that given below:

1. Reading of the minutes of the previous meeting.

2. Points arising from these minutes and their signing as a true record.

3. Chairman's opening remarks.

4. Financial matters.

5. Motions for discussion and voting. (These should appear on the agenda, if possible and supporting documents should have been read, previously.)

6. Date for next meeting.

7. Any other business. (For minor matters.)

Minutes should contain: the date and place of meeting; the members present and accurate, unambiguous accounts of the discussion items and resultant decisions. The amount of detail recorded depends on the importance of the subject matter and tradition. Some minutes are almost a verbatim record, others give the bare minimum. Minutes usually follow the same order as the agenda, are in the past tense and are numbered.

# *The Nutron Factor*

As a Divisional Sales Manager of a large cosmetic and toiletries firm, you receive the following letter from your Central Office. Read the letter carefully, answer the questions which follow it and then take the appropriate action as requested.

## Costol Cosmetics Ltd

### Costol House
### London N1

June 1st, 19—

Dear (Yourself),

I enclose the sales figures for our latest hair-conditioning cream, "Nutron". Have a look at them and see what you think:

| Age of Purchaser | 14–24 | 25–34 | 35–44 | 45–54 | 55–64 | 65–74 | Sales represented in per thousand sold. |
|---|---|---|---|---|---|---|---|
| February | 1 | 1 | 2 | 2 | 2 | 0.5 | sold. |
| March | 1 | 1 | 4 | 3 | 2 | 0.6 | Age breakdown calculated by "Opinion Research" |
| April | 5 | 3 | 5 | 4 | 3 | 0.8 | |
| May | 2 | 4 | 6 | 5 | 3 | 2 | |

The sales drive in March boosted the April sales but all the advertising was directed at the late-teenage market and I am not sure that this was a good idea. I think a return to the "health-centred" advert might be better: "Nutron gives lift and vitality to hair – protects against extremes of weather – prevents drying and splitting." This kind of thing should bring better results, especially considering the time of year.

In connection with the Nutron Sales Drive, I have a very important job for you. We have approached Miss Serena Sahi, the immensely wealthy Pakistani model and starlet, in the hope that she will consent to feature in our advertisements for Nutron in Pakistan. We are very keen to make an impression on the market since the upper-class Pakistani ladies have always used hair-cream as a protection for their hair from the sun. Ours being a rather more sophisticated and feminine version of their local preparation, we could do very well – especially if the packaging is fairly luxurious. Miss Sahi will be visiting us at Head Office at the end of June and we hope to finalise contracts without delay. She has an enormous personal following and her recommendation will make all the difference to our sales figures.

While in England, Miss Sahi particularly wants to visit one of our factories and also to spend some time in "a typical English town". Thus, the obvious solution is to send her to you in (insert name of your own town or city) for the day, on 27th June, then you could quickly show her round the factory in the morning and take her out on the town in the afternoon. We will put a car and chauffeur at her disposal so that you could go out into the country – if you wish – but do remember that Miss Sahi has to be back in London for a late dinner and that the mile or so from our factory to the centre of town can become very congested after about five o'clock.

Miss Sahi's manager will be travelling with her and luckily he speaks good English (Miss Sahi's is somewhat limited). Also, they are both vegetarians but that should not present too much difficulty as long as you go to a good class hotel for lunch. I do feel, however, that you should contact the manager of one of the better hotels beforehand, just to make sure that they will waive their "no ladies-in-trousers" rule. (Although Miss Sahi dresses flamboyantly, to say the least, she is a good Moslem, wears the traditional tight trousers and top, NOT a sari). The most important thing is to make sure that nothing untoward happens since I have heard that she is rather temperamental and we could lose the contract if she is offended.

As soon as you have thought for a bit, send me a detailed account of how you propose to spend the day and your suggestion as to some present we can give Miss Sahi to mark her visit. Sorry to burden you with all this; I know you are dreadfully busy. Perhaps you should comfort yourself with the thought that she is certainly the most beautiful official visitor you are likely to have for some time!

Expecting to hear from you in a week or so,

CHARLES TOWNSEND
Marketing & Advertising Manager

**Exercises**

1. (a) How would you describe the tone of Charles Townsend's letter? What particular phrases and vocabulary give credence to your view?

(b) With reference to the sales figures, why does Charles feel that a further advertising campaign for the teenager is not a good idea? Where might one more profitably direct advertising?

(c) Why is the health-orientated advertising particularly appropriate for the time of year the letter was written? How might his health-type advertisement improve sales in general?

(d) What reasons has Charles for believing that the sales to Pakistan might be high?

(e) What does Charles Townsend mean by the expression: "enormous personal following"?

2. Send details of your proposed itinerary for the day to Charles Townsend, explaining why you have decided on certain excursions rather than others and making provision for bad weather. Also give your preference as to the present Miss Sahi should receive. The names of hotels, restaurants or whatever should be real as should the siting of the factory in comparison to the town centre. Maps and other reference books should be used so that no impossible distances or closed museums mar Miss Sahi's day. (If details on local places of interest and their opening times are difficult to obtain – a list of people to contact to discover such information should be given. If you are a long way from London, then arrangements may have to be made for Miss Sahi's arrival by train and her departure by this means or bookings will have to be made in a local hotel so that she can travel back the next day, having had dinner in your town on the evening of her visit.)

It would help Charles Townsend if you could also recommend reference books which give some facts and figures on Pakistan so that Colston's do not appear ignorant of or uninterested in Pakistani affairs.

3. Write a letter, confirming an earlier telephone call, to the manager of the restaurant or hotel where you have booked lunch for the 27th, explaining the rather extraordinary circumstances and forewarning him of Miss Sahi's special needs.

4. Having heard of Miss Sahi's forthcoming visit, the Pakistani workers at your factory are planning a demonstration to coincide with her tour. They complain that while a quarter of the work-force are Moslems, the present rigorous time schedule prevents their stopping work to pray so they would be much happier working flexi-time. (Colston's factory employees work from 9 a.m. to 5 p.m. with one hour for lunch and a 15 minute break, morning and afternoon. Office staff sometimes stay after 5 but there is no evening or night shift on the production line.)

They also complain that several female Moslems have had their applications for promotion turned down on the grounds that all lady supervisors, managers or administrators are required to wear 'suitable business attire' when at work and this excludes either the trousers or long skirts which Moslem ladies wear for modesty's sake.

To avert this demonstration, you, as Personnel Manager call a meeting to which you invite the Moslem spokesman, the Production Manager, Sales Manager and a union representative. Conduct this meeting *once all the participants have mustered information on flexi-time, Islam and the legal precedent for insisting on certain types of clothing at work.*

## CHECK LIST FOR QUESTIONNAIRES

Before putting pen to paper, decide whether *quantity* or *quality* is the most important.

*Quantity*
In your assignments you are not usually expected to decide how many people to question or whether these people are truly representative since choosing a fair sample for questionnaire distribution is specialised work. However, quantity is important when you are constructing questions because each answer will have to be checked, thus, a straight Yes/No or Box-Ticking format might be for the best where the sample is large enough to strain your checking resources.

*Quality*
If you need suggestions or feelings rather than facts then a neat, Yes/No format may be useless. Open-ended questions, eg "Have you any suggestions for future activities?", take more checking and often give less clearly categorisable results but they allow people to express any reservations. (Asking a question twice, from slightly different perspectives, can sometimes lead to more balanced answers too.)

## THE QUESTIONNAIRE

1. People need encouragement to spend time answering a questionnaire, so explain why answering helps those questioned or offer a free gift, etc.

2. Only ask for personal details if these are necessary and show tact over matters of income and age.

3. Find out how valid answers are by asking key questions early, eg a questionnaire on attendance at dentists might have "Do you wear dentures?" high on the list.

4. Avoid leading questions, eg "What do you like about living in England?"

5. Avoid ambiguous questions by keeping questions short and by taking extra care with pronouns, eg "If they were to become a nuisance, what do you think they should do about them?", is likely to confuse the reader.

6. Where a questionnaire is distributed by post, instructions for its return and a closing date may be necessary.

In general, presentation is very important since a cramped or confusing layout is very off-putting. Try and maintain an overall system of boxes or ticks, or written answers, etc.

Before beginning the first questionnaire, the group could look at examples of questionnaires from magazines and consider the conflicting claims of anonymity and accuracy (see 2. above).

# The Battle for Manston

1. Compose a report to the Manston Council from the Roads Sub-Committee, using information from the attached documents and following these terms of reference:

    "To determine the views of interested parties on the proposed rerouting of the A27, from Burley to Manston via the grounds of the Manor House."

2. The Council having received the report of the sub-committee, feel that the general public's views were inadequately represented. You have therefore been asked to prepare a questionnaire to be distributed to the residents of Manston. The Council wishes to know how much public support, if any, the proposals enjoy, and in particular, whether the views of the Manston Preservation Society and Chamber of Commerce are popular.

3. Write a letter from the Council to Lt-Col R H Rambling, MC outlining the alternative proposal made by the Preservation Society and asking for his views on it.

4. Imagine that the alternative proposal has been decided upon. The Council, in view of the considerable public interest in this project, have decided to issue a press release explaining the reasons for their final decision. Write this to a limit of 250 words.

---

## Document A

Press Release by the Manston Preservation Society

The gardens of Manston Manor, towards which the local council is extending its rapacious claws, are recognised by connoisseurs as being amongst the finest examples of the early work of Reuben Hay (1601-1683), later gardener to the royal family. The V shaped lawn bordered by flowering shrubs and bisected by a single straight drive is typical of Hay and illustrates perfectly his love of simple, yet dramatic, effects. The magnificent prospect of the Manor as seen from the main gates has been called "one of the most photographed views in England", and its great popularity with the manufacturers of greeting cards and calendars has given it a prominent place in the heart of English people everywhere.

It is this remarkable view that the council wishes to destroy. If the proposals recently made public are ever carried out the main Manston to Burley road will be diverted to run directly through the celebrated lawn. The Council have chosen to ignore our alternative suggestion and to continue with their desecration of this unique portion of our heritage for no other purpose than to allow motorists to proceed at ever increasing speeds from one unfortunate village to the next.

Can any true son of Manston, or of England, remain unmoved by this hideous piece of official vandalism? The Manor House lawn was lovingly laid three centuries before the pompous philistines who planned this scheme were ever born. Left to itself it will delight the eyes of Englishmen for as long a period again.

---

# Document B

A letter to the Manston Argus

Dear Sir,

May I use your columns to express my thanks to those many local people who have pledged their support to the "Save Manston Lawn" movement. I am sure that they will be interested to know that they have been joined in their protest by thousands of others from overseas. I have received letters from North America and from the furthest corners of the commonwealth, many enclosing cheques or assurances of financial aid should that necessity arise.

I need hardly say how moved I have been by this expression of public support. Three years ago I hesitated before taking the decision to open the doors of my ancient home to the public in an attempt to defray the extortionate demands of the exchequer. When I see now how many good friends have been won for Manston by this policy I can no longer doubt its wisdom.

Yours faithfully,

Lt-Col R H Rambling, MC

# Document C

Selections from Interviews with Residents of Manston

*Mr L Brown*   I live not 100 yards away from Manston House Corner and I hold my breath every time I hear a car go around that bend, and for every accident that does happen there's a dozen more near misses.

*Mr J Richards*   You can say it's the driver's fault the first time an accident happens anywhere, but when you get accidents once a fortnight you must begin to suspect the road as well.

*Mrs D Thomas*   If you'd seen some of the things I've seen after an accident on that corner you'd not worry over much about the bloody lawn.

*Mrs A Jones*   The children will hang about the Manor gates during the summer to see the visitors arrive. It's only a matter of time before one of them is killed.

*Miss G Thirsdy*   I think I speak for most of the older people in the village when I say that we just don't know what to decide. We don't want to lose the lawn, but we can't put up with these dreadful accidents.

# Document D

Summary of Interview Undertaken by Sub-committee with Spokesman for the Manston Chamber of Commerce, Mr A Sellars

Mr Sellars has statistics to prove that since the Manor House was opened to the public in 1969, there has been a considerable increase in local trade, both in the vicinity of the house itself and in the town at large. He points to several new shops which have opened on the strength of the increased passing motorist trade, including two garages on the Burley-Manston stretch of the A27. Several cafes and hotels in the town have reported a boom in business during the summer months over the past two years.In short, the opening of the Manor House to the public has greatly increased the scale of the tourist industry in this somewhat depressed area. There is, in Mr Sellars' opinion, no doubt that the closing of the Manor House grounds would cause this tourist trade to fall off thus depriving the town of a valuable source of revenue and employment which it could ill afford to lose.

# Document E

| Accident Figures | 1980 | 1981 | 1982 | 1983 |
|---|---|---|---|---|
| Number of vehicles using A27 per day in July | 382 | 431 | 673 | 951 |
| Number of accidents at Manor House corner per year | 9 | 10 | 18 | 21 |
| Total number of accidents on A27 each year | 14 | 16 | 23 | 24 |
| Number of paying guests admitted to the Manor House | | | 15,873 | 24,034 |

| Nature of Accidents at Manor House Corner | 1980-1983 |
|---|---|
| Loss of control over vehicle | 42% |
| Collision with stationary vehicle | 38% |
| Injury to pedestrians or cyclists | 15% |
| Others | 5% |

# Document F

<u>Map Showing Alternative Schemes</u>

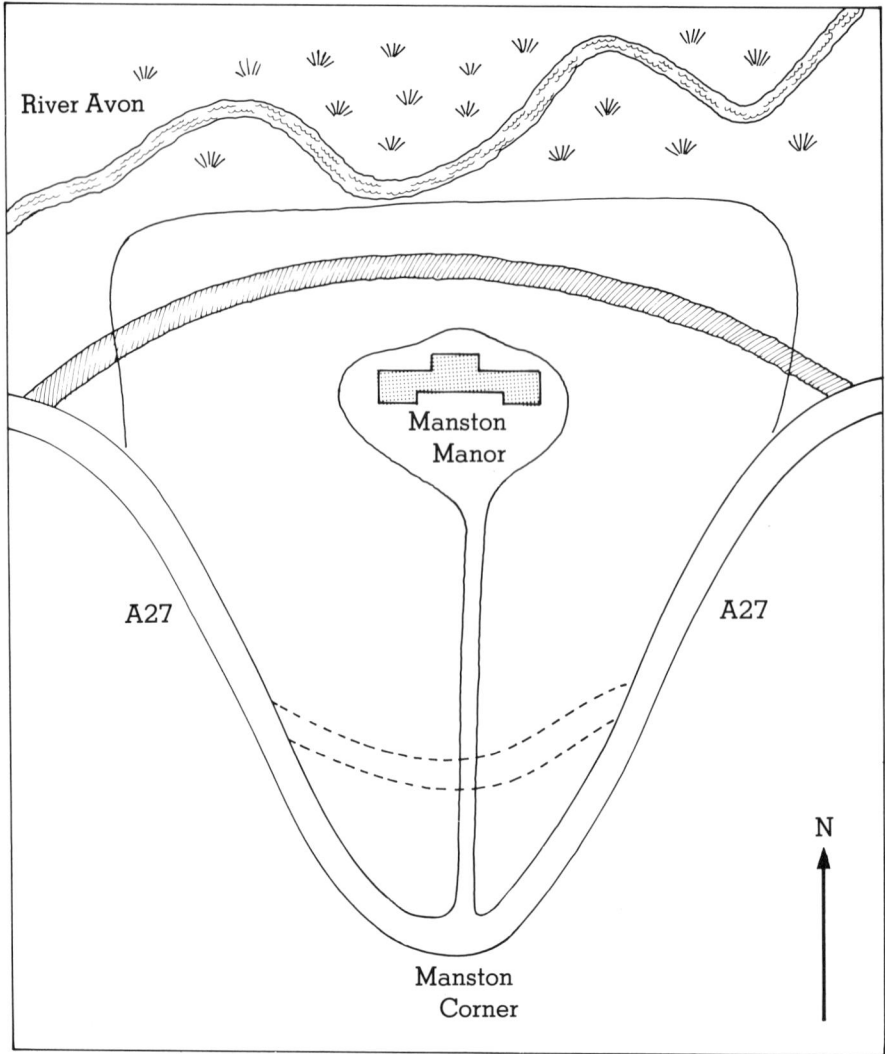

- – – – – – Council's Proposed Route

- ▨▨▨▨▨ Preservation Society's Alternative Route

- \|// \|// \|// Marshy Ground

CHECK LIST FOR INTERPRETATION OF STATISTICS

1. Note any general trends and try and give reasons for them.

2. Pick out any exceptions to the general trend and try and give reasons.

3. Work through each division of the statistics in an orderly manner (chronologically or alphabetically, etc depending on the axes of the statistics). Note any internal general trends and exceptions and try and give reasons.

4. If the statistics seem unclear or limited, point to the consequent ambiguities and outline those areas where further investigation might be useful.

5. Write up neatly, keeping associated points together.

   This same logical approach should be adopted in all factual writing; the analysis of maps, photographs or diagrams being undertaken from left to right, or from major detail to minor detail, etc. This accurate step-by-step approach may be practised by describing a mechanism or process, which you know about through your work, to someone for whom such knowledge is new, eg:

1. Describe: a franking machine, a chemical fire extinguisher, a computer terminal.

2. Explain how a Roneo duplicator works.

3. Describe three types of filing systems.

# *Welcome to Avondale Leisure Centre*

You are employed as an Assistant Manager (Admin) at the Avondale Leisure Centre, a local authority amenity which was opened in 1976. It had never been intended that the Leisure Centre should be a profit making organisation, but it was expected to break even, or at least to operate without substantial aid from the Authority. This has not happened and in the present climate of austerity the Authority has ordered an examination into the operation of your organisation with a view to cutting the deficit.

Printed below are instructions to you from Mr D C Fields, the General Manager of the Centre. Carry out these instructions with the aid of Documents A to D which follow.

1. I understand that you have completed your analysis of the Centre's financial position and of the contribution made by the major activities to that position. (The information is contained in Document A, which represents the results of your analysis.) Write me a report summarising the main trends indicated by these figures and making any recommendations you see fit. Keep statistics to a minimum, I want a clear, overall picture, not a mass of figures.

2. I enclose a letter which I received this week (Document B). Mr Hardy has a point, I think. We did decide not to send out reminders this year because of the increased postal charges, but the fall in subscription revenue is most marked as your figures show. In view of this I have decided to resume the

practice of sending out reminders as from the end of this month. I want you to do two things:

(a) Write a letter to Mr Hardy thanking him for his comments and informing him of our decision.

(b) Draft a circular letter to all members who allowed their subscriptions to lapse during the period when we did not send out reminders. We really need those subscriptions so a simple reminder won't do, remind them of the benefits we offer. (Information relating to subscription rates can be found in Document C).

3. I have been in contact with the Editor of the *Avondale Argus* who has agreed to do a feature on the Sports Centre. The presentation will be primarily photographic, but he would like a brief article, only about 500 words, on the facilities offered, the cost, etc. Please write this article using the leaflet (Document C) as a guide.

4. I hope you have a complete set of notes on the decision taken at the Admin. meeting yesterday (you have, see Document D). I want you to prepare the initial publicity material for the competition, namely a leaflet to be distributed locally giving details of the competition and stating clearly who are eligible to enter and what will be expected of them.

Secondly, design a poster to attract attention to the competition, but without most of the details which will have been included in the leaflet. The printers will handle the design of both pieces, but your draft should obviously show the general layout you anticipate.

# Document A

| ANALYSIS OF THE CENTRE'S FINANCIAL POSITION | | | | | |
|---|---|---|---|---|---|
| | 1979 | 1980 | 1981 | 1982 | 1983 |
| Membership Subs. | 60,000 | 80,000 | 72,000 | 74,000 | 67,000 |
| Fees | 300,000 | 320,000 | 318,000 | 310,000 | 290,000 |
| Total Income | 360,000 | 400,000 | 390,000 | 384,000 | 357,000 |
| Expenditure | 340,000 | 380,000 | 400,000 | 410,000 | 410,000 |
| Balance | + £20,000 | + £20,000 | –£10,000 | –£26,000 | –£53,000 |

| FACILITY | No. of Participant Hours | Income | Cost of Upkeep |
|---|---|---|---|
| Outdoor soccer pitches | 280,000 | £40,000 | £45,000 |
| Squash and badminton courts | 90,600 | £90,000 | £12,000 |
| Tennis courts | 4,320 | £35,000 | £10,000 |
| Hire of Sports Hall | 255,000 | £55,000 | £45,000 |

# Document B

---

9 Paddock Way,
Avondale.

3rd May, 198—

The Centre Manager,
Avondale Sports Centre,
Bridge St.,
Avondale.


Dear Sir,

    I enclose a cheque for £4.00 to cover my family's membership of the Leisure Centre for the coming year.

    My Membership Card No. 13642 expired six weeks ago and I was surprised not to receive the usual reminder. I assumed this to be merely an oversight but several friends who had been members of the Centre for some years confirmed that they had not received reminders either.

    If this is a new policy I can only suggest that it is extremely unwise as I know of several other people who have allowed their membership to lapse.

                  Yours faithfully,


                  Oliver Hardy

---

# Document C

AVONDALE SPORTS CENTRE
BRIDGE STREET
AVONDALE

DIRECTOR:  Mr D C Fields

Telephone:  Avondale 6363/4

Membership Annual Subscription:  £2.50 per person
£4.00 per family (Parents plus all children under 17)

Payment may be made by post (Cheques sould be made payable to Avondale C.C. and crossed "Sports Centre Account") or at the Centre's reception desk. Day membership is available to members' guests at a cost of 25p.

An additional fee is payable for each activity. This fee varies according to the activity and full details are given in a separate leaflet available from the centre.

Sports clubs and other groups may hire the Sports Hall and outside pitches for their own activities on payment of a Group Membership Subscription of £5.00.

Other Facilities

A crèche staffed by qualified children's nurses is available during the day for parents wishing to leave infants while they use the centre's facilities. A charge of 10p per child is made for a maximum stay of two hours.

The Centre Cafe serves snacks and drinks throughout the day and evening.

Sporting goods may be purchased by members at a special discount price at the Centre Sports Shop – open 9.00 a.m. – 5.30 p.m. daily.

The following activities are provided at the Centre.
Members are requested to book in advance.

Archery (Monday 7-9 p.m.)
Basketball (Monday 7-9 p.m.)
Golf Practice (Tuesday and Thursday 7-9 p.m.)
Cricket Nets (March to September, any evening)
Football (September to June. Bookable at any time)
Five-a-side Football (September to June. Bookable at any time)
Hockey (September to June. Bookable at any time)
Squash (Bookable at any time)
Badminton (Bookable at any time)
Tennis (Bookable at any time)
Weight Training (Friday 7-9 p.m.)
Judo (Tuesday and Wednesday 7-9.30 p.m.)
Physical Fitness (Men Wednesday 7-9 p.m.)

A public swimming pool is situated on the Sports Centre Site, to which members are admitted at reduced rates.

# Document D

Proposed "Superlad and Superlass" Competition.

Minimum age 17 years.

All competitors to compete at the following sports:

Badminton, Squash, Gymnastics, Running, Weightlifting (men only), Standing Long Jump (ladies only,) a variety of Physical Exercises.

Prizes: 1st   £150 of Sports Equipment (three prizes for men and three for women)
       2nd   £75   of Sports Equipment
       3rd   £40   of Sports Equipment

Each prizewinner will receive free life Membership of the Centre.

The competition will be held during the week beginning 19th June. Heats on Monday, Tuesday, Wednesday.

Eliminators on Thursday and Friday and Grand Final on Saturday

Other attractions – displays by first class gymnasts each evening – John Goody, the Avondale-born England soccer player, will introduce the finalists and present the prizes.

Application forms from the Centre Office.

Entry Fee 50p

Crowning of Miss Leisure Centre 198— —applications as above, no entry fee.

## CHECK LIST FOR MEMORANDA AND OTHER PRINTED STATIONERY

Many offices use printed stationery for such communications as memoranda or telephone messages. This practice increases efficiency since there is less to write and the layout of the stationery encourages a concise and standardised approach.

```
┌─────────────────────────────────────────────────────┐
│                   MEMORANDUM                          │
│                                                       │
│  To .....................    Subject.................  │
│                                                       │
│  From ................       Date ..................   │
│                                                       │
│                                                       │
│                                                       │
└─────────────────────────────────────────────────────┘
```

*A typical printed memo pad*

### MEMO CHECK LIST

1. Be as concise as possible by using numbering and phrases rather than flowing sentences.

2. It is not necessary to sign a memo or to use a salutation or a complimentary close.

3. Do not forget:

   (a) Memos are usually unsolicited. (Certainly a request for something more detailed may require a report.)

   (b) It may be considered rude to send memos to superiors: 'Memos down, letters up'.

```
┌─────────────────────────────────────────┐
│              TELEPHONE                    │
│                                           │
│  To: .................   Date: .........  │
│                                           │
│  From: ...............   Time: .........  │
│                                           │
│                                           │
│                                           │
│  Taken by: .............................  │
└─────────────────────────────────────────┘
```

If these details are not printed *you must* include them.

*A typical printed telephone pad*

# TELEPHONE MESSAGE CHECK LIST

1. Write clearly.
2. Be accurate, especially about action required.
3. Have telephone pads handy and forward any messages as soon as possible.

If possible, use the internal telephone system of the college to practise accurate communication by telephone. The class could be divided into 'Student Enquirers' and 'College Administrators' and they could use the entry requirements, enrolment procedure and course content of their present BEC course (which the Student Enquirer hopes to join in September) as their information content.

'Students' and 'Administrators' should elicit all necessary information from each other and notes should be made where further action is required either by the parties involved or by some other party.

The 'Administrators' might find a copy of the College Prospectus useful and, both 'Students' and 'Administrators' should accept that the enquiry is made in late May.

# CHECK LIST FOR NOTE-TAKING AND NOTE-FORM PRESENTATION

(The notes given as background information in the following assignment are inefficient and you will need to use the following check-list and your summarising skills to use them effectively.)

Where notes are to be used at some later date or where they are for the benefit of other people, the note-taking process has three distinct stages:

1. Get all necessary information.

Cues in the spoken word: voice change in the speaker, the speaker summarising for you. Listen for phrases such as, "Now, to sum up . . ." or "There are three main differences", etc. Also listen for direct questions.

Cues in the written word: similar summarising phrases such as those above, plus, the subject of a paragraph is often outlined in the first sentence of that paragraph.

2. Tidy up.

Remove repetitions.
Bring together points which are associated.
Remove examples and anecdotes (unless the notes are to be used as an aide-mémoire, in which case short reminders may be left, eg 'joke about mother-in-law', 'pause for laughter', etc).

3. Presentation.

Use headings and numbering.
Give each new point and sub-point a new line.
Read back over the notes and see if they make sense in themselves.
Provide a reference to the original by giving the name of the author or speaker and stating where and when the speech was delivered or the article published.

# The Problematical Playgroup

Having heard that there are very few facilities for the under-fives in Heathcote, a local resident has offered part of her house for use as a pre-school play-group centre.

Your chief is interested in the venture put forward by Miss Lovatt-Jones (Document A) but would like some more detailed information on *who needs the service and why*. As an experienced member of the Council's clerical staff, you have been asked to prepare a questionnaire to be distributed to the residents of Heathcote.

You may find the following suggestions useful:

1. Are babies to be catered for?
2. Is a full or half-day service required?
3. Would support in the form of funds be forthcoming?

You are also asked to compose a report to Heathcote Council using the information from Miss Lovatt-Jones' letter and map including recommendations. Your chief suggests that this report should:

> "determine the suitability of 'Green Acres' for use as an All-day Play-Group Centre, with especial regard to existing facilities which would need changing and those additional facilities which would be necessary."

Your chief realises that such schemes rarely run smoothly and asks you to talk to the Chief Education Officer to find out what difficulties *he* anticipates (Document B). Naturally, you must make Miss Lovatt-Jones aware of all your findings, but you are warned that the letter you write should take into account her goodwill and that it must not be too discouraging.

Write the letter.

A lady Councillor has heard of the scheme and regards it as 'retrogressive'. She sends you the results of a recent survey, to prove her point (Document C). In the form of a memo, send a verbal account of the findings to your chief.

## Document A

Green Acres,
Heathcote,
Notts.

13th June, 198—

Dear Sir,

I have recently been left a property in your area and wish to put it to some good use. At present, I live entirely on the first floor of this substantial house with the housekeeper of my late uncle. Whilst I never married, I have always been fond of children and, after reading in the local press of the need for a Pre-School Playgroup, I decided that I could offer you the lower half of my house for this purpose.

Although I am in my late fifties, I am pretty active and would love to help; along with other volunteers, who I am sure would be forthcoming. I have trained as a nurse and, during the war, I taught in a temporary school for evacuees in Yorkshire.

Whilst I can offer my services and my property, I have very little cash available with which to equip the building and had hoped that you would defray the initial cost and running costs from public funds. (These should not be great since, despite its length, the main hall is comfortably warm when the two fires are lit.)

I attach a sketch-map of the ground floor*. The garden is walled on three sides, only the front of the house opening on to the road, but it would probably be best for the children to use the side gate (which leads onto the Great North Road) since the main drive leads away from the town.

Yours faithfully,

Emilia Lovatt-Jones

*See Document D

## Document B

Notes on the Conversation with the Chief Education Officer, Regarding Playgroups (presented to you by his secretary).

Such schemes have failed because:-

takes ages to sort out rotas for transport etc
householder may not be as able as she thinks
may have uncertain knowledge of what is involved
the local Council Estate is pretty rough
may feel a stranger in her own house
where the householder is elderly already she may soon regret her commitment or be unable to fulfil it
may not agree to structural changes in house
voluntary help may soon flag
the scheme means a great deal of noise
deterioration of property
many 'unsavoury' children and mothers . . . is Miss L-J a Lady Bountiful?
will take some time to implement . . . may feel discouraged
mothers may resent her as benefactress
lack of privacy
may object to council checking her credentials and looking into her past
the house and garden will look very different if scheme goes ahead
not a move to be contemplated in haste.

# Document C

## The Survey Sent by the Lady Councillor

Groups of five children of the same age but from different backgrounds and circumstances, were given a vocabulary test in which they were asked to put 100 well-known words into sentences of their own to show that they knew the meaning; for each word used correctly, they scored one mark.

### Children at Home

|                      |    |    |    |    |    |
|----------------------|----|----|----|----|----|
| Middle glass girls   | 92 | 95 | 90 | 90 | 90 |
|                      | 90 | 91 | 95 | 89 | 91 |
|                      | 89 | 91 | 94 | 93 | 89 |
| Middle class boys    | 85 | 93 | 85 | 90 | 84 |
|                      | 84 | 86 | 92 | 85 | 84 |
|                      | 84 | 87 | 84 | 85 | 86 |
| Working class girls  | 84 | 84 | 88 | 81 | 83 |
|                      | 83 | 82 | 85 | 90 | 81 |
|                      | 82 | 87 | 82 | 85 | 85 |
| Working class boys   | 78 | 78 | 81 | 80 | 80 |
|                      | 80 | 81 | 80 | 79 | 73 |
|                      | 76 | 80 | 75 | 78 | 76 |

### Children in Semi-Residential Nurseries

|                      |    |    |    |    |    |
|----------------------|----|----|----|----|----|
| Middle class girls   | 85 | 85 | 86 | 85 | 82 |
|                      | 83 | 84 | 81 | 85 | 89 |
|                      | 83 | 81 | 86 | 84 | 86 |
| Middle class boys    | 80 | 77 | 77 | 78 | 76 |
|                      | 80 | 78 | 76 | 77 | 81 |
|                      | 76 | 77 | 78 | 80 | 80 |
| Working class girls  | 78 | 78 | 78 | 79 | 79 |
|                      | 80 | 76 | 79 | 78 | 78 |
|                      | 79 | 78 | 76 | 82 | 76 |
| Working class boys   | 72 | 74 | 75 | 74 | 73 |
|                      | 78 | 75 | 74 | 74 | 70 |
|                      | 76 | 72 | 78 | 70 | 72 |

# Document D

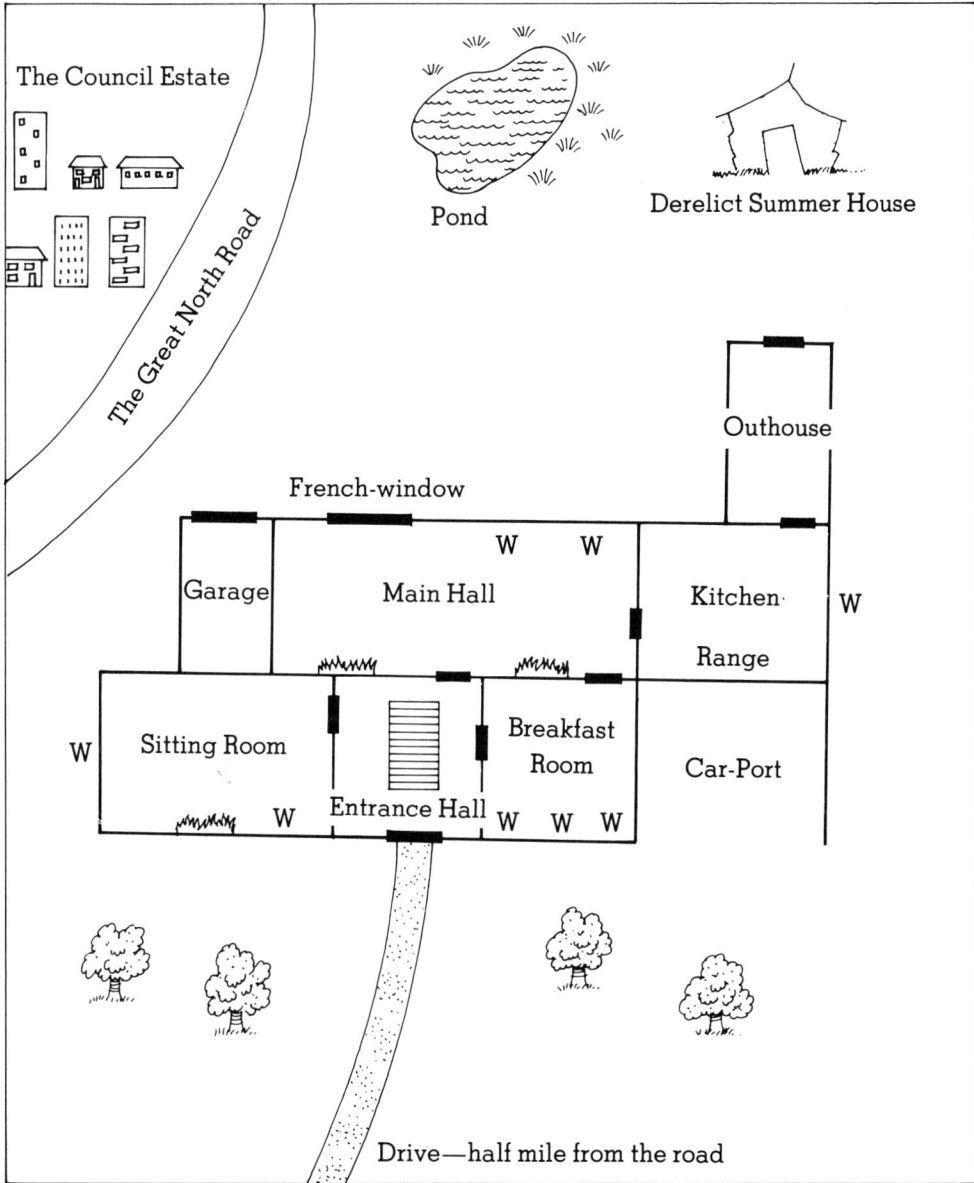

The Council Estate

The Great North Road

Pond

Derelict Summer House

Outhouse

French-window

Garage

Main Hall

W    W

Kitchen

Range

W

Sitting Room

W

Entrance Hall

Breakfast Room

Car-Port

W    W    W

W

Stairs

Drive—half mile from the road

Door

W — Window

Open Fire-place

Marshy Ground

Stairs

51

# The Oak Holme Defence League

The residents of the Oak Holme Housing Development have protested against a proposed plan to build a residential centre for mentally handicapped children on a five acre site adjacent to their homes. They have pursued their campaign vigorously since the Council's first announcement of the scheme six months ago and what should have been a source of pride to the Council is rapidly becoming an embarrassment to some councillors.

Printed on the pages following, you will find the documents listed:

1. The results of a survey carried out by the Oak Holme Young Mothers' League (Document A).
2. A press statement issued by the Young Mothers' League (Document B).
3. A letter to the press written by a County Councillor who lives in Oak Holme (Document C).
4. A highly confidential note from the Roads and Bridges Department (Document D).
5. A memorandum from the County Surveyor (Document E).
6. A memorandum supplied by the County Medical Officer of Health who is very eager to see that the Centre is built as planned (Document F).
7. A map of the proposed development (Document G).

Your task is to find how the Oak Holme Young Mothers' League has managed to put itself in the position of the injured party and to reverse this situation by any means possible. Use the M.O.H.'s memorandum as the basis of your argument but remember that the opposition has proved expert at manipulating public sympathy and that you may be forced to do the same thing. Form yourselves into a Health Department Sub-Committee to discuss the situation and produce the required counter propaganda.

---

## Document A

Results of a Survey Carried out by the Oak Holme Young Mothers' League within a Two-mile Radius of the Proposed Centre

| | |
|---|---|
| Number of people questioned | 5,320 |
| Number of people opposing the scheme | 5,072 |
| Number of people without an opinion | 217 |
| Number of people in favour of the scheme | 31 |

Those interviewed were asked to read a copy of the Young Mothers' League press statement in order to familiarise themselves with the facts and were then asked to express an opinion of the project.

# Document B

Press Statement issued by the Oak Holme Young Mothers' League

The residents of the Oak Holme Residential Development feel that it is their duty to bring to the public's attention some serious flaws in the proposed plan for building a Residential Centre for Mentally Handicapped Children at Eade House. We have every reason to fear that this fine project might turn out to be the cause of immeasurable tragedy if the plans are not changed. Our fears are based upon three main points which are outlined below.

1.  Access to the new Centre will be from the B1573, a very busy road as we in Oak Holme know to our cost. We protested against the upgrading of this previously unclassified road two years ago but to no avail, and since that time it has become a source of danger to our children. God forbid that children not in complete control of their faculties should ever be allowed near this public racetrack. Should children stray further afield (and who can stop children wandering?) their parents may well be faced with the hideous task of identifying their shattered bodies, for the main Bidwell road is less than a mile distant.

2.  The River Eade which will run through the proposed Centre would be a pleasant amenity to many institutions, but surely a fairly deep river is the last thing any sensible person would wish to see in the grounds of this particular Centre.

3.  The flood basin of the Eade begins just behind the proposed Centre and is a treacherous expanse of marshland which even normal children have been known to find dangerous – yet another opportunity for a tragic accident.

The parents of Oak Holme live with these dangers daily and we know of the anxiety they cause. We feel that to expose the parents of handicapped children to similar conditions is a monstrous crime.

# Document C

Letter from County Councillor Sibly to the Eade Chronicle

> Sir,
>
> I wish to applaud the public spirit shown by the Oak Holme Young Mothers' League in revealing the stupidity of the Council's proposal to build a Centre for Mentally Handicapped Children at Eade House.
>
> I would like to add my own comments to theirs. I have long been an admirer of Eade House, a superb example of Elizabethan architecture, the noblest architecture, in my opinion, to be produced in this country. Though regrettably derelict, the house is not beyond repair and several local businessmen have speculated on the possibility of turning it into a country club where residents of the area can relax from the cares of their daily work. The river would be an asset to such an institution and the road no more of a danger than it is now. We would enjoy the spectacle of a magnificent building restored to its former grandeur. Instead, Eade House

is to be demolished to make way for yet another glass and concrete monstrosity, and a monstrosity agreed by every sane person to be sorrily misplaced at that.

The people of Eade must make their feelings felt on this subject immediately and the most effective way of doing so is to write to local councillors asking for an undertaking not to support the scheme. If the opposition is strong enough our Council will know what has to be done.

Yours etc.,

A R Sibly

## Document D

Comments from the Roads and Bridges Department (Highly Confidential)

If it were possible to charge a collection of people for lying, the Oak Holme crowd would be guilty indeed. According to our records, and we do fairly regular surveys, the B1573 carries less traffic than any other comparable road in the county. It is really no more than a country lane and as far as we know there has never been an accident on it.

As for that fool Sibly, his precious Eade House is a ghastly mock Tudor affair built by a local margarine magnate during the 1930's. It was more or less gutted by fire shortly after the owner had lost his business on the gambling table. The Insurance Company paid up with very bad grace if I remember properly.

## Document E

### MEMORANDUM

**From:**   The County Surveyor

**To:**   (Yourself)                    **Date:**   13th November, 198—

Subject: Eade Marsh

Eade Marsh is certainly designated as a flood area on Ordnance Survey maps and technically it is the flood plain of the River Eade. The last time the Eade overflowed its banks was in 1563 and the event was rare enough then to be entered in the Parish Records. I am informed by the competent authorities in my department that the designation "Swampy Area" is an anachronism and I know from personal experience that the entire area is as dry as a bone.

# Document F

**MEMORANDUM**

**From:**   The Medical Officer of Health

**To:**   (Yourself)          **Date:**   13th November, 198—

Subject: Eade House

Do those people think we are all fools? The children would be well looked after and never allowed to leave the Centre grounds unattended. The river will be fenced off and the children will not be allowed near it without adequate supervision.

We really need this Centre. The county's only other institution at Brimson, is bursting at the seams. It has been a tremendous success but the demand for places is naturally growing along with population growth.

# Document G

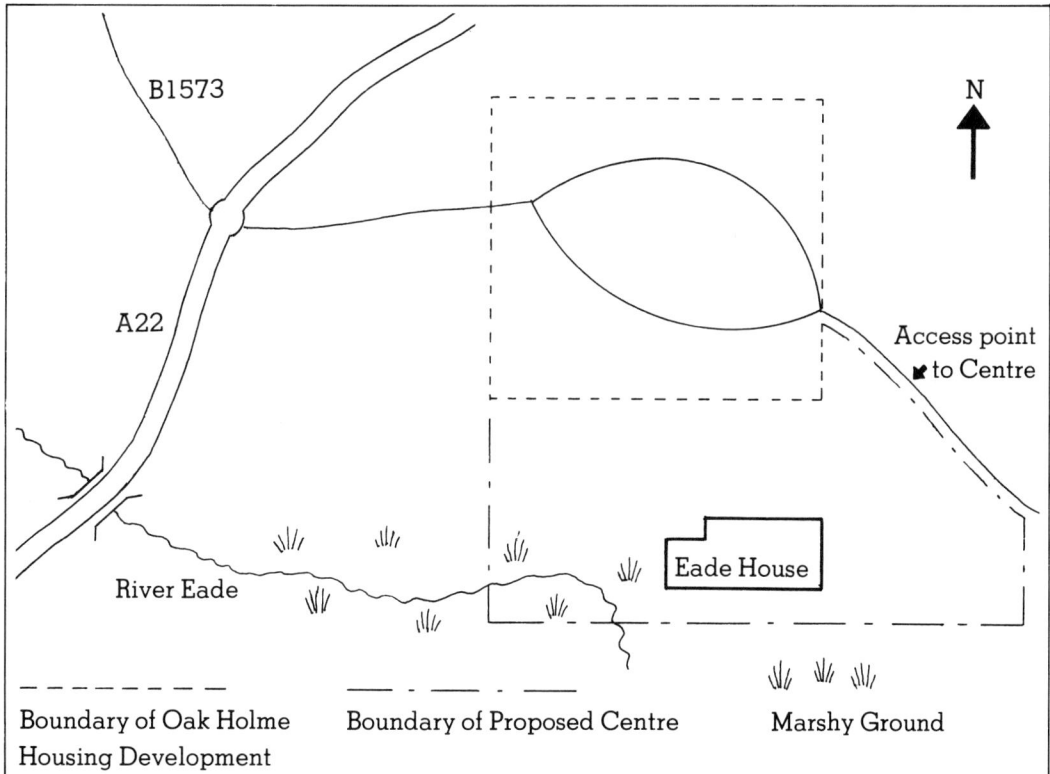

B1573

A22

N

Access point
to Centre

Eade House

River Eade

- - - - Boundary of Oak Holme     — · — · — Boundary of Proposed Centre     Marshy Ground
Housing Development

# Tough Toys

You are Assistant Sales Manager to Tough Toys Ltd – a small but thriving toy firm. Their latest venture is self-construct toys. The idea is that the toys are produced in kit-form; the customer then assembles the pieces himself, thus cutting out labour costs and making a considerable saving. The finished toy should represent a high standard of workmanship and yet be approximately 30% cheaper than comparable fully-constructed toys.

The Firm intend this first self-assembly toy to be a fort. They have made trial forts in three different materials but it has not become clear which of these materials would be most suitable. The Managing Director, therefore, asks for a report to be compiled to help him come to a decision.

The Firm decide to adopt your recommendation for the fort, and sales, promoted on the basis of 'Quality and Economy', are going well. Criticism of the fort by customers would be most harmful at this stage, however; so that when several letters arrive complaining about missing wing nuts you are asked to deal with the matter personally. You investigate and discover that the wing nuts are packed by machine and that this machine sometimes overheats and stops delivering wing nuts. Usually this fault is corrected immediately but some kits must have got through to the customer.

**Exercises**

1. Using the information provided in Document A produce a report for presentation to the Directors and Finance chiefs, outlining the advantages and disadvantages of the various materials you would recommend them to use in their production of a fort, for the $3\frac{1}{2}$ to $5\frac{1}{2}$ year old market.

2. Reply to the letter from Mrs James (Document B) explaining what steps you have taken to ensure that this mistake does not happen in the future, doing everything possible to counteract her poor opinion of the firm.

3. The Sales Manager will be attending the Amsterdam Toy Fair during the last week of January, thus the rather nerve-wracking task outlined in Mr Wellbeloved's memo (Document C) falls to you.

   a. Produce the speech, in note form (and deliver it to the class, if possible)

   b. Send a memo to the Accounts Section of Tough Toys, suggesting the kind of expenses you are likely to incur during the trip to Brighton and asking them to make funds and other necessary facilities available.
   (For the purpose of calculating travel arrangements, you may presume that Tough Toys' factory is situated next to your college. If you can drive and choose to go by car, provide the Accounts Section with an approximate mileage. If you cannot drive, provide the Accounts Section with detailed public transport costs and think again about the samples!)

56

# Document A

Dear . . . . . .

    I hear that you have been asked to prepare a report on the proposed fort kit. I enclose an excerpt from on article showing toy-buying trends, which you might find useful – especially when considered in conjunction with the facts and figures compiled during our testing of the trial forts.

The best of luck!

James Wellbeloved

<u>From an Article by Dr Kidd ('Society Now', November 1983) entitled 'Christmas Shopping for Children'</u>

. . . More toys are now being produced in "natural fibres" – wood, rafia, cotton etc. This is to 'cash in on' the nostalgia trend in buying habits, which was noted by Dr Weaver in his article 'Backwards to Sales Progress' ('Society Now', May 1983). Parents are pleased to buy these toys – not only because they are beautifully finished but because they hark back to that Victorian childhood which has begun to stand for all that was good and wholesome. These toys are usually very sturdy and, because of their simplicity, are enjoyed by children from 3 to 7 years. Large toys in natural fibres do tend to be expensive but they last a lifetime and are amazingly accurate and convincing.

Younger children prefer more garish toys, preferably ones that also make a noise. The market here is dominated by the Japanese. They can produce polythene, plastic and thin metal toys far more cheaply than the British and despite complaints from retailers and customers about shoddy workmanship, there is still a large demand. Parents do seem prepared to spend more if the toy will last but with very young children variety is important and parents will not invest large sums of money on toys which will soon become redundant.

While being initially attracted by bright exciting-looking toys, older children soon tire of those which leave no scope for investigation or imagination and are scornful of inattention to detail – particularly enjoying to-scale models.

One interesting fact which emerged from our survey was that fewer and fewer children receive surprises for Christmas – most parents are given very definite 'orders' by their children as to which presents will be acceptable and toys are no exception.

Results of the Trials on the Self-assembly Fort

The three materials tested were: metal, wood and heavy duty polythene.

Cost to Customer

Metal £12
Wood £8
Polythene £6

Amount of detail possible (graded 'Very High' to 'Very Low')

on    Metal — High
      Wood — Moderate to High
      Polythene — Low

N.B. With the metal forts, greater detail did create a safety problem since sharp edges became unavoidable unless the metal was 'bonded' – which doubles the price. (The polythene was the safest material, of course.)

Colour preference for the fort – by age group:

|  | 2 – 4 years | 4 – 6 years | Parents |
|---|---|---|---|
| Bright blues and reds, etc | 70% | 35% | 30% |
| More realistic and subtle colours | 30% | 65% | 70% |

N.B  The heavy duty polythene holds vibrant colours well but subtlety cannot always be guaranteed.

# Document B

'High Gables',
Fleetwood,
Deanshire.

May 11th 198—

Production Manager,
Tough Toys,
Hampton Road,
Grindshire.

Dear Sir,

I recently bought my son one of your self-assembly forts for his birthday. My husband and I spent an evening putting the pieces together and were pleasantly surprised at the clarity of the instructions and the excellence of the pieces.

Everything went well until the final stages of construction when we discovered that 6 wing nuts used to fix the turrets and draw-bridge were missing. Because of this fault we were unable to complete the fort and had to present it to our son in a shoddy and makeshift fashion.

I admit that buying the fort in kit-form cuts the price, but surely this type of error could be avoided. We would hope that you will send us six suitable wing nuts, without delay – and we suggest you find out why the kits are being sent out without being checked.

Yours faithfully,

Julia James (Mrs)

## Document C

### MEMORANDUM

**From:** Mr Wellbeloved      **Subject:** Conference, Jan 31st

**To:** Assistant Sales Manager      **Date:** Jan 2nd

We have been invited to send a representative to the Small Firms' Conference at the new Brighton Centre on 31st Jan. The Sales Manager will be away at that time, but I am sure you will 'fit the bill' admirably.

They want a short talk – suggested title, 'Quality not Quantity' – with two main elements:

1. Some idea of Tough Toys policy in developing the self-construct fort.
2. A personal view of the type of contribution a small firm such as ours can make to British Industry and any suggestions as to what the Government could do to encourage our type of initiative.

Don't forget to take a few samples and some advertising 'bumf' – you never know who will be there!

Best of luck

J W

# *Education Cuts*

You are employed as an Assistant to the Director of Education, Newshire County Council. Your duties are principally concerned with passing information to the Director and with keeping interested parties informed of his views.

Like many other Local Authorities, Newshire is facing an unprecedented financial crisis. Every conventional economy measure has already been taken, but the Education Department has been ordered to cut another £100,000 from its budget by any means possible. The Director of Education, after consultation with senior members of his Department, has devised two alternative schemes whereby this saving could be achieved.

**Exercises**

1. Read Document A which outlines the proposed schemes and write the letter as requested for the Director's signature.

2. The Director feels that the views of the parents are crucial in this matter and asks you to prepare a questionnaire which will be distributed to a 10% sample of parents. It is intended both to inform these parents precisely of what the two schemes entail and to discover which scheme has most support and why. It will, of course, be useful to know whether the parents work, how many children they have at school and the ages of these children. Remember that you will have to collate the results of this survey in a very short time with a small staff.

3. The response to your letter to the schools (Question 1) is immediate and dramatic. (See Documents B and C). Write a report to the Director summarising the points made and the action taken by the National Union of Public Employees and the Teachers' Unions as reported in the *Newshire Express*. The aim of the report is to brief the Director prior to his meeting with Union representatives.

4. A decision has been taken by the Director and you are informed of this in a meeting with him. He asks you to prepare a statement for the press explaining the decision and giving the reasons for it. In Document D you will find notes taken by yourself during a meeting with the Director. Use these as the basis of your answer.

5. Mr H Worthy, Senior County Adviser for English, has written a memo to the Director (Document E). The Director approves of Mr Worthy's suggestions and orders you to write a circular letter to be sent to all Educational Advisers asking them to attend a meeting at County Hall on a date and time to be decided by you. The purpose of the meeting should be made clear in the letter.

# Document A

**NEWSHIRE COUNTY COUNCIL**

**Memorandum**

**To:** (Yourself)                    **Subject:** Expenditure Cuts

**From:** Director of Education       **Date:** 25th June

---

Outlined below are two schemes either of which, it is estimated, will save
the Department about £100,000. Write a letter to all school Heads asking
for their comments, and those of their staffs, on which scheme they would
prefer to see put into operation.

1. The pupil/teacher ratio to be altered as follows:

|                   | Present Ratio | Proposed Ratio |
|-------------------|---------------|----------------|
| Secondary Schools | 17 to 1       | 17.5 to 1      |
| Primary Schools   | 23 to 1       | 23.5 to 1      |

2. An additional week's holiday to be taken at Christmas and Easter. The
   saving would be made from the wages of ancilliary staff and heating
   and lighting costs.

Stress the grave financial position and make it clear that one or other of
these schemes will be adopted, so what we want is constructive advice.

# Document B

Report in the 'Newshire Express'

## SCHOOL CANTEEN WORKERS ANGRY

Newshire Schoolchildren may get an extra week's holiday at Christmas and Easter, but the
cost saving measure has angered canteen workers and cleaners who claim it will cost them
money.

The Director of Education said that saving on heating and lighting alone would be about
£50,000, but hundreds of ancilliary workers in Newshire's 300 schools claim they will lose
cash when they most need it – at Christmas.

The National Union of Public Employers will be taking up these grievances with Newshire
County Council. Union Organiser David Selway said, "The Education Department has failed
to appreciate the total effect of these cuts on the community. Not only will our members be
losing money, but thousands of working mothers will have to stay at home during the
extended holidays."

# Document C

Report in the 'Newshire Express'

## TEACHERS' ACTION HITS NEWSHIRE SCHOOLS

The Education Committee's plan to increase the pupil teacher ratio in Newshire schools has provoked an angry response by the Teachers' Unions who believe that about 50 jobs will be axed next year.

On receiving news of the proposal, the National Association of Schoolmasters 1000-strong county branch immediately threatened classroom chaos in protest against the cuts.

They refused to take classes for colleagues absent for more than one day at five comprehensive schools and threatened similar action in 20 other schools.

The 3000-strong branch of the National Union of Teachers is expected to take similar action if its officers are not informed, at a meeting with the Director planned for next week, that the scheme has been abandoned.

Mr John Saunders, County Secretary of the N.A.S. said, "We oppose any tampering with the pupil/teacher ratio because it could prove difficult to get the Education Department to reverse such a move at a future date. If cuts have to be made we favour the alternative scheme of giving extra holidays at Christmas and Easter because the public will be fully aware of what is happening and will keep pressure on the Education Department to revert to normal holidays as soon as possible."

# Document D

Notes of your Meeting with the Director

Decision – Longer Holidays. Pupil teacher ratio to be left alone. Extra week at Christmas and Easter.

Decision taken on advice of Head teachers who see longer holidays as less harmful educationally.

Sorry about loss of earnings to ancilliary staff, but better than sacking 50 full time teachers.

Hope employers will prove co-operative re working mothers during longer holidays.

Results of your questionnaire show parents would prefer change in pupil – teacher ratio – less disruptive where both parents work. Try to convince them otherwise.

Stress educational needs paramount – future of our children and community at stake.

# Document E

NEWSHIRE COUNTY COUNCIL

**Memorandum**

**To:** Director of Education      **Subject:** Extended Holidays

**From:** H Worthy      **Date:** 8th July

I am concerned about the position of pupils in the final year of examination courses. It is these who are most likely to suffer from the extended breaks. I suggest that you call a meeting of Advisers to discuss methods of overcoming the problem as soon as possible.

## CHECK LIST FOR LISTENING TO AND PRESENTING AN ARGUMENT

The following assignment will involve you in listening to the views of other people and presenting your own.

When a person speaks, his message may be made less clear because of:

1. External interruptions.
2. The speaker's failure to give reasons for opinions expressed.
3. The speaker's failure to keep to the point, by:

repeating himself,
making unhelpful comparisons and digressions,
developing his argument in an illogical manner,
using steps in his argument which do not necessarily follow.

These faults may not be under the speaker's control so the listener will have to remain alert and ask any necessary, clarifying questions.

Messages also become distorted by the use of false arguments (used, intentionally or not). Thus, the listener must be able to recognise:

1. Unprovable and/or subjective claims.
   eg "Your staff will enjoy using our product because of its handsome appearance . . . etc."
2. Flattery.
   eg "Such a system would present no difficulty to your hardworking and experienced staff."
3. Arguments which depend totally on their emotional appeal (and use rhetorical questions).
   eg "To deny a child this book is to deny him happiness – and who could deny a child happiness?"
4. Arguments which use comparisons which are only partially true.
   eg "Working with the general public is very like fighting a battle – a losing battle."
5. Arguments which depend upon vague generalisations.
   eg "This system has been introduced in America to great effect."

There is a place for emotional and non-rational argument, in that the clever use of humour, pauses, subjective language and charm may improve a case *which has a sound basis, anyway;* but downright false claims may be detected and you can actually cloud your argument and leave yourself open to suspicion if you do not let an idea 'sell itself', to some extent.

In general, when presenting an argument, you should:

1. Assess your audience.
   Would technical terms speed your delivery to your audience, flatter your audience, or baffle your audience?
   Would humorous touches, relax your audience, confuse your audience or antagonise your audience?

2. State your general position and, if possible, alert your audience to the major steps in your argument.

3. Use simple sentences; and provide any helpful visual aids.

4. Provide evidence for your statements and have further instances *speedily* at your disposal, if necessary.

5. Summarise your argument.

6. Listen to questions or responses carefully. Suggest other sources, when an answer is outside your knowledge or scope. Note weaknesses in opponents' arguments and be ready to counter-attack.

To practise these skills:

1. Listen to recordings of parliament and analyse the speeches with regard to their information and presentation.

2. Listen to professional interviewers and the way they frame questions.

3. Compare several newspapers' accounts of the same incident.

4. Compare different advertisers' methods of promoting similar products.

5. As a class, complete the Committee Game outlined, below – and remember to discuss what you have learnt, afterwards.

# "Decisions, Decisions, Decisions . . ." (A Case Study in Local Government Finance)

This is a role playing assignment intended to allow students to practise committee work and to give them some understanding of the problems which have to be solved at policy making level. The assignment is not, of course, intended to bear any relation to the way in which local authorities actually distribute money.

The assignment is in three parts:

1. A student or group of students is allocated to each committee and asked to prepare a case, based on the notes, to favour his committee's recommendations. These cases are then discussed in the main committee.

2. A break is taken during which alliances may be made between departments with similar aims.

3. The main committee then allocates the funds available according to the effectiveness of the revised claims presented by individual or allied departments.

# DEPARTMENTAL BUDGET PROPOSALS

| Committee | Project | Cost (£) | |
|---|---|---|---|
| Highways | 1 Road Widening Scheme | 450,000 | |
| | 2 Roundabout | 90,000 | |
| | 3 Multi-storey Car Park | 250,000 | |
| | | | 790,000 |
| Transport | 4 Repair Depot | 150,000 | |
| | 5 Bus Station | 100,000 | |
| | | | 250,000 |
| Children | 6 Children's Home | 65,000 | |
| | | | 65,000 |
| Premises | 7 Planning Department | 45,000 | |
| | | | 45,000 |
| Education | 8 New Primary School | 100,000 | |
| | 9 Comprehensive School | 250,000 | |
| | 10 Youth Centre | 40,000 | |
| | 11 Technical College | 200,000 | |
| | | | 590,000 |
| Fire | 12 New Fire Station | 50,000 | |
| | 13 Houses for Firemen | 75,000 | |
| | | | 125,000 |
| Health | 14 Ambulance Garages | 15,000 | |
| | 15 Mental Health Adult Training Centre | 80,000 | |
| | 16 Health Centre | 60,000 | |
| | | | 155,000 |
| Library | 17 New Branch Library | 40,000 | |
| | | | 40,000 |
| Welfare | 18 Home for the Aged | 120,000 | |
| | 19 Hostel for the Elderly Mentally Infirm | 90,000 | |
| | | | 210,000 |
| Housing | 20 Blocks of Flats | 810,000 | |
| | 21 Housing Estate Extension | 250,000 | |
| | | | 1,060,000 |
| | | | 3,330,000 |

SUM ACTUALLY AVAILABLE £2,000,000

# Notes on Departmental Claims

1. <u>Highways Committee</u>   Road Widening Scheme

The main road which runs between Newtown and Commuterville (A0123) has been built to dual carriageway standards throughout the eleven miles of its length, except for two miles to the east of the village of Bullingly. Apart from commuter traffic in the morning and evening, there is considerable general and heavy traffic along this road throughout the day. Serious traffic jams occur on the single carriageway section and a number of accidents have occurred there. It is proposed, therefore, to re-align this two mile section of road and build it to dual carriageway standards.

Cost: £450,000

2. <u>Highways Committee</u>   Roundabout

The junction of Post Road (A021), Hill Road and Little Lane is causing considerable concern because of the traffic delays occasioned by this complicated intersection. Traffic lights have not eased the situation and, at certain times of day, traffic may be delayed for up to an hour. A careful study of this situation and an examination of similar situations and their solutions in other parts of the country have been made by the Committee. The ideal solution would be to build flyovers and associated slip-roads, but the cost of such a project would be considerable. With this in mind, the Committee have endeavoured to find a solution where the cost would be reasonable. It is proposed, therefore, that a roundabout and associated road works should be built to ease traffic flow at this intersection.

Cost:  £90,000

3. <u>Highways Committee</u>   Multi-storey Car Park

The parking problem for private traffic in the centre of Newtown has once more reached proportions where immediate, effective action in essential if all traffic in the centre of the town is not to come to a standstill. The Highways Committee have, in fact, in the past few years undertaken a number of projects to ease this situation, but because of the limited finance available each exercise has merely been a short term solution. The Committee now propose that a multi-storey car park be built to house 500 cars. If certain traffic restrictions were imposed to ensure that motorists used the car park provided by the authority a gross income of between £15,000 and £20,000 p.a. could be envisaged.

Cost: £250,000

4. <u>Transport Committee</u>   Repair Depot

The repair and maintenance of the Authority's vehicles (except buses and other associated vehicles) has been carried out at a central repair depot for twenty years. The number of vehicles and plant has increased from under 500 when the depot was established to over 1,500 now. The depot has been expanded on its present site several times but this has never been entirely satisfactory. The depot is very difficult to work because it is a series of small units, the accommodation is cramped and there is restricted storage space and the general efficiency and productivity of the depot is limited. The Transport Committee propose that a new site on the outskirts of Newtown should be purchased and a new repair depot be built where it can be properly planned and where there would be space for further expansion when necessary.

Cost: £15,000

5.   Transport Committee   Bus Station

The Central Bus Station was built on a limited site shortly before the war. It was possible to expand it on its present site because of buildings which had been demolished by bombing, though this was done on a piecemeal basis as the situation demanded. The result is that the present bus station is not satisfactory because it has never been planned as one unit. Also the accommodation for drivers, passengers, etc, and for the administration of the bus station is very limited and, to a large extent, housed in unsatisfactory prefabricated units. It is proposed therefore to rebuild the bus station on its present site. By doing so it would be possible to improve the efficiency of the bus station and to accommodate at least twice the present volume of traffic without increasing the actual area of the bus station.

Cost: £100,000

6.   Children's Committee   Children's Home

The Committee have for some time wanted to provide residential accommodation for children in care in the Riverside district. The main problem has been to find a suitable site in this area. However, a number of older properties could be adapted to provide the necessary accommodation. We propose, therefore, that three adjacent properties be purchased and that they be rebuilt, decorated and furnished to provide residential accommodation for 15 children. The Home would also provide accommodation for the residential staff necessary.

Cost:  £65,000

7.   Premises Committee   Planning Department

The Planning Department was originally housed in part of the Municipal Offices but when expansion took place it was moved into a house which was converted for such use. Since then further expansion has taken place and other properties have been taken over to house various sections of the department. The present situation is one where eight separate properties are being used, some of them being most unsuited to this purpose. This is not conductive to efficiency and a great deal of time is wasted by a staff having to move from one building to another in order to carry out their work. A site has recently become available near the municipal offices and the premises committee propose that a two storey building should be erected on this site to accommodate the Planning Department as it is at present established. The site is one which would allow for further expansion when this becomes necessary in future years.                                                                        Cost:  £45,000

8.   Education Committee   New Primary School

A new primary school with a capacity for 200 children is needed to relieve pressure on four existing schools. Extensions to several housing estates has made the problem critical.

Cost: £100,000

9.   Education Committee   Comprehensive School

Under the Council's plan for secondary education King William's Grammar School will be expanded to form the new comprehensive school. The money is required for additional classrooms. The scheme has been approved by the DES and cannot be altered.

Cost: £250,000

10. Education Committee    Youth Centre

A lack of amenities has been blamed for the high level of vandalism on the Council's
Kingsmead Housing Estate. It is proposed to provide a building and basic amenities;
decoration and provision of other amenities will be undertaken by the club members.

Cost: £40,000


11. Education Committee    Technical College

The local Technical College has built up an excellent reputation and now wishes to offer
more advanced Engineering courses for which there is a great demand from local industry.
The considerable sum of money involved will provide a new and highly sophisticated
engineering workshop to house these courses.

Cost: £200,000


12. Fire Committee    New Fire Station

The existing fire station cannot adequately meet the needs of a growing town. This is a
relatively cheap scheme for its size because the Council already owns land with a suitable
building on it and much of the equipment will be salvaged from the old station.

Cost: £50,000


13. Fire Committee    Houses for Firemen

The eight new houses proposed will, it is hoped, both improve recruitment to the brigade
and help provide better fire cover as they will be situated adjacent to the new station if it is
built.

Cost: £75,000


14. Health Committee    Ambulance Garages

Two of the Health Department's fleet of very expensive ambulances lack garage facilities
and are, according to an inspector from the transport section, likely to deteriorate and
become increasingly unreliable if they are not properly looked after. It is proposed to build
two garages incorporating equipment for routine maintenance.

Cost: £50,000


15. Health Committee    Mental Health Adult Training Centre

This is a new project which will make use of experience gained in other Authorities. The aim
of the project will be the rehabilitation of mentally ill patients and their return to work.

Cost: £80,000


16. Health Committee    Health Centre

It is proposed that four medical practices serving the North of the town be housed in a new,
purpose built health centre. In the opinion of the Medical Officer of Health a far better
service could then be made available to a large number of patients.

Cost: £60,000

17.  Library Committee   New Branch Library

The much expanded Kingsmead Estate is situated three miles away from the nearest County Library. At present the area is served by a mobile library but many complaints have been received of the total inadequacy of this service. A new branch library is proposed on ground adjacent to the estate.

Cost:   £40,000

18.  Welfare Committee   Home for the Aged

Over half of those who apply for a place in one of the Council's existing Homes die before they get there because of the very long waiting list. This sum would enable the Committee to house a further 40 old people in comfort and safety, almost eliminating the waiting list in one stroke.

Cost: £120,000

19.  Welfare Committee   Hostel for the Elderly Mentally Infirm

These patients are either treated in hospital, where they occupy valuable beds for very long periods, or at home by relatives whose lives are always dominated and often ruined by the demands made on them. This Hostel would be used for long term stays by patients with no one to care for them, and for shorter stays by others in order to lessen the load on their relatives.

Cost:   £90,000

20.  Housing Committee   Blocks of Flats

The Committee wishes to build three new blocks of flats on a site at the edge of the county town. A total of 120 flats would be built in medium rise blocks. This project would go a long way to improve on the Council's dreadful housing record.

Cost: £810,000

21.  Housing Committee   Housing Estate Extension

This project is the last phase of the three stage expansion of the Kingsmead Estate and would complete the Council's present building programme. Twenty-five new houses would be built.

Cost: £250,000

Note: you are only concerned with the capital cost of the projects and may assume that running costs, staffing, etc have already been covered.

# *Poison In Our Midst*

As a management trainee for Chalfont's, the specialists in water-proof clothing, you have been working in the personnel department for six months and have been mostly concerned with schools' liaison. Therefore, when what seems to be a fairly innocuous complaint from a group of schoolchildren (Document A and B) arrives, it is passed on to you for reply.

Do not deny Chalfont's part in the pollution but point out that this extra chemical waste is a by-product of a new process which Chalfont's have been forced to undertake in order to compete with Japanese manufacturers. Inability to compete in world market would mean redundancy for many of Chalfont's 700-strong work force – 75% of whom are Waltham people.

One of the children's parents has written a letter to the local Press under the heading, "Poison in our Midst" (Document C) and it has caused great public alarm. Since you were involved in the original reply to the children and have been cited in Mr Dodds' letter, you have been invited to speak on local radio.

Prepare a 5-10 minute talk explaining the actual extent of pollution on the Twane and pointing to the most likely sources. Your talk should reassure the inhabitants of Waltham and, to that extent, the false arguments and subjective comments made by Mr Dodds will have to be identified and repudiated but you do not want your talk to become a personal attack on Mr Dodds.

Deliver the talk.

(Chalfont's could agree to take part in a pollution 'phone-in' immediately after your talk. If this 'phone-in' materialises, appropriate questions from the public, a compère, Mr Dodds and Mr H F Chalfont will be necessary.)

Research and describe the policy regarding complaints *where you work at present, or within your educational institution.* You will need to consider internal complaints as well as complaints from the public and whether the complaint is directed at a person, a product or a service. Your description could be partly diagrammatic or incorporate a flow chart.

What is your present employer's attitude toward statements to the Press – or radio? (Full-time students should regard the Education Department as their employer.)

Using your own work experience, or the results of an enquiry to a large local firm, state which members of staff would be kept informed about a complaint concerning public safety.

# Document A

Science Dept.,

Waltham School,

Waltham.

Dear Sir,

    We, the undersigned, under the supervision of our Biology Mistress have been testing the River Twane, at six points, for pollution.

    Our tests (enclosed) reveal an alarming amount of industrial waste – a fact supported by the lack of fish in the water – and we were wondering if you would take action to prevent possible danger to the public and to make the river a nice place to go, again. At the moment, foam and dirt can be seen floating on the water while the shallows are littered with old cans and various other rubbish.

              Yours faithfully,

              Jane Tabor
              Timothy Dodds
              John Greenway

Encl              etc

# Document B

The Children's Findings

| Latest reading at the six points on the Twane (see below). | | | The previous year's readings at the six points on the map. | | |
|---|---|---|---|---|---|
| 1. | 1.4 | None | 1. | 1.3 | None |
| 2. | 1.5 | 0.9 | 2. | 1.3 | 0.3 |
| 3. | 2.6 | 0.9 | 3. | 2.0 | 0.3 |
| 4. | 2.8 | 1.0 | 4. | 2.2 | 0.3 |
| 5. | 5.8 | 1.4 | 5. | 5.5 | 0.6 |
| 6. | 5.9 | 1.4 | 6. | 5.7 | 0.6 |
| | A | B | | A | B |

A = Foreign Matter
B = Chemicals

These figures are entirely fictitious to avoid complexity.

The number given above represents cc per litre. Water is considered fit for drinking when there are fewer than 2 cc of foreign matter in a litre and when *all* chemicals are absent. Water is considered dangerous to humans when there are over 10 cc of foreign matter to a litre and more than 3 cc of chemicals per litre.

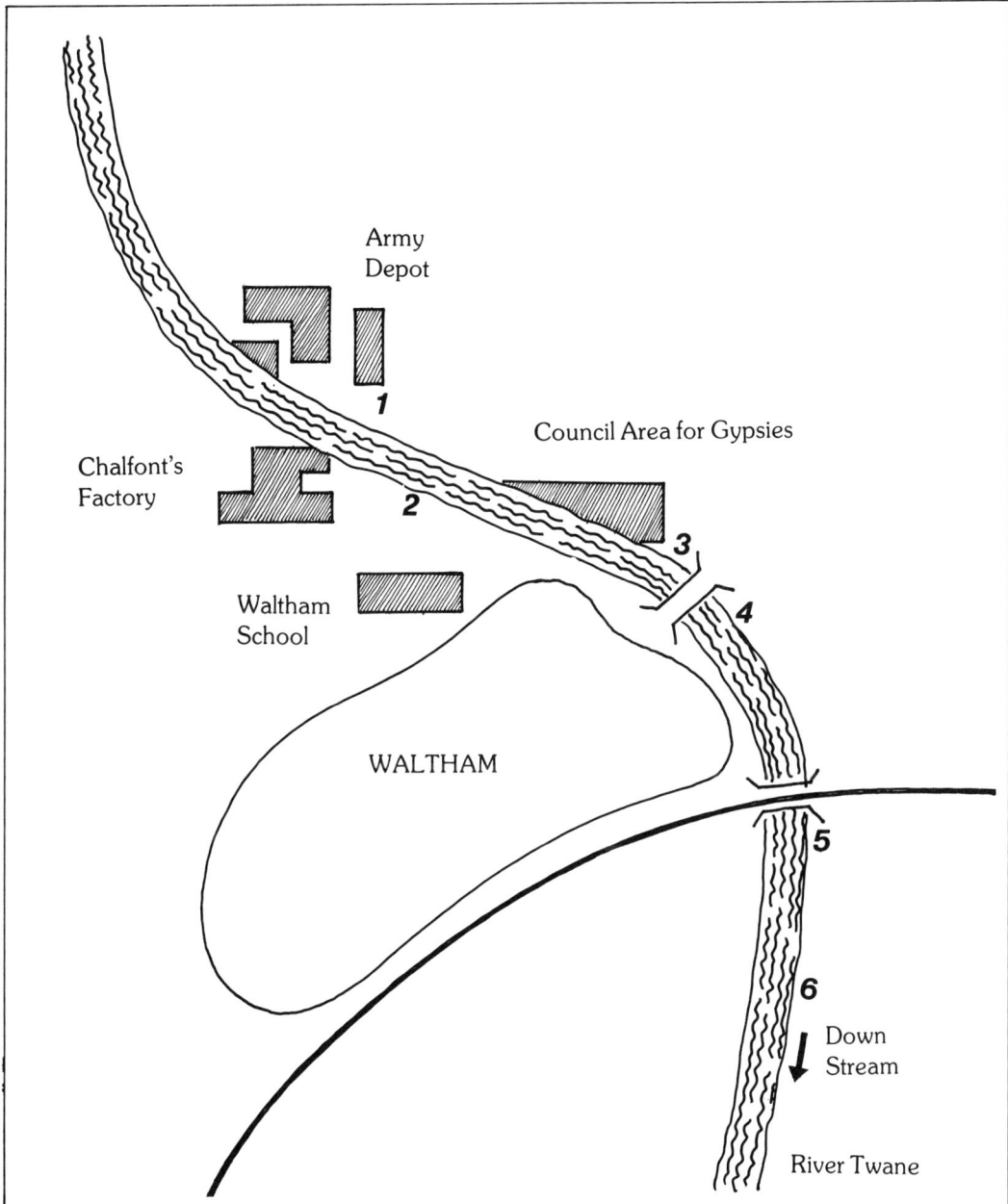

Army
Depot

1

Council Area for Gypsies

Chalfont's
Factory

2

3

4

Waltham
School

WALTHAM

5

6

Down
Stream

River Twane

# Document C

POISON IN OUR MIDST!

The River Twane is now polluted to an unacceptable level. Rubble and household rubbish proliferates along the banks and the fish are fast disappearing. Chalfont's, whose waste is contaminating this once pleasant waterway, are closing their eyes to the situation; just as the authorities at Aberfan closed their eyes . . . How many need to die before something is done?

I remember a time when the Twane was full of trout. Nowadays, you are lucky to see the odd gudgeon. Last year, the pollution level doubled and at this rate, the water will be so contaminated in five years' time that people living near the banks of the river will have to evacuate their homes. No wonder Chalfont's management do not live here in town. They don't want to subject their children to untold risks. It is Waltham people who suffer. And what do Chalfont's give to these unofficial guinea-pigs in return? I remember a time when the A259 was a mere by-road and when you could see green fields even from Waltham High Street. Chalfont's management lives behind nice high hedges and up long expensive driveways, no-one goes littering their backyards, yet the normal people of Waltham have to put up with Chalfont's garbage on their very doorsteps. They have lost their birthright for Chalfont's profits.

The view of the river from the road bridge was once famed. Now it is marred by swirls of noxious foam on the water and the rotting hulks of prams and paint pots rearing out of the stagnant shallows.

Like me, many residents of Waltham fought in the War for a free country. A green and pleasant land to bring our children up in. But Chalfont's deny us that freedom. Big business is dictating how we should live. When my child showed me the letter which he received from Chalfont's in reply to the school science department's complaint about the growing menace (out of the mouths of babes and sucklings!) I was enraged. No real apology was forthcoming and the job of fending off this propitious criticism was given to some underling who signed him or herself . . . (your name) . . . pp Mr H F Chalfont. What do Chalfont's mean entrusting something of this nature to someone who is probably still wet behind the ears? Are Chalfont's disguising the real state of affairs by fobbing off the citizens of Waltham with some half-baked reply? These questions must be answered. Insist on your rights as ratepayers and parents. Don't let Waltham become just another item on 'News at Ten'. Act now!

Mr L B Dodds

# Fire Down Below

You are employed as an Administration Officer by the Newshire Fire Authority with special responsibility for personnel management.

In common with most other Fire Brigades, Newshire finds difficulty in recruiting sufficient part-time firemen (technically known as Retained Men). As these men are the backbone of the Brigade in a predominantly rural area, the efficiency of the service is seriously threatened.

On the instructions of the Chief Fire Officer, you have prepared a questionnaire and issued it to all part-time firemen. The aim of the exercise was to discover the types of men who come forward for this duty and their motives for so doing.

The questionnaire and a summary of the replies are given in Documents A and B.

**Exercises**

1. Write a report to the Chief Fire Officer summarising the conclusions to be drawn from the replies given in Document B and making any recommendations you see fit.

2. Document C is a letter which, three years ago, was circulated to households situated within two miles of Fire Stations in the hope of recruiting part-time firemen. No replies were received. It was written by an elderly officer of somewhat inflexible views. Produce a new letter incorporating as much of the information given in the original as you think relevant and giving any further details from other documents which you believe should be included.

3. (a) Produce the notice referred to in the Chief Officer's Memo (Document E). Remember that it must be unambiguous, likely to interest its readers, but at the same time, specific as to the conditions attached to the offer.

   (b) Write the letter to Station Officers referred to in Document E.

4. As a result of your campaign, you are beginning to receive telephone enquiries from potential Retained men, asking for more details and checking on various aspects of the work. Make yourself familiar with all the documents, especially Document E and make such a call, either as the Administration Officer or as an Enquirer.
   (If there is no access to internal telephones, this summarising element of the assignment could be completed, verbally, by writing an article of about 500 words for the *Newshire Herald* on the subject of the part-time fireman's work, with a view to attracting young men to the part-time fire service.
   The points raised during your meeting with the Chief Fire Officer (Document E) would be particularly useful here.

# Document A

NEWSHIRE FIRE AUTHORITY

QUESTIONNAIRE TO BE COMPLETED BY ALL RETAINED MEN

1. Year of Birth                                                    19

   Year of First Joining the Service                                19

2. Marital Status on Joining the Service          Married/Single

   Number of children on Joining the Service          _____

3. Type of Employment on Joining

   (a) Were you self-employed?                          Yes/No

   (b) What were your normal hours of work:          _____hrs. per day

   (c) Were there any other retained firemen at your place of
       employment?                                          Yes/No
       If so, how many?                                     _____

4. Classification of Employment on Joining

   (a) Manual ☐  (b) Clerical ☐  (c) Professional ☐

5. Social Activities on Joining

   Were you at any time before joining a member of any of the
   following organisations?

   Youth Club ☐ College ☐ Sports Club ☐ Social Club ☐

6. Educational Background

   How old were you when you left school?                    _____

   Any educational certificates (GCE, CSE, etc) _____

7. What were your reasons for joining the service? Indicate the
   order of importance of the following points to you by placing the
   numbers 1 to 5 in the boxes provided.

   (a) Thought the work would be interesting  ☐

   (b) Sense of social responsibility  ☐

   (c) Financial reward  ☐

   (d) Comradeship and social activities  ☐

   (e) Services Background  ☐

8. How was the service brought to your attention?

   (a) By word of mouth                                _____

   (b) Recruitment Advertising                         _____

   (c) Witnessed the service in action                 _____

   (d) Read Press Reports                              _____

# Document B

Total Number of Replies 105

## Question 1

Age on joining the service

| | |
|---|---|
| Below 20 years | 25 men |
| 20–22 years | 38 men |
| 23–25 years | 27 men |
| 26–28 years | 12 men |
| 29 + years | 3 men |

## Question 2

83 of the men were married on joining the service.
52 of these had at least one child.

## Question 3

a. 23 men were self-employed.
b. Normal working day in the main. The work does not attract shift workers.
c. 75 of the men worked with at least one other retained man.
d. The vast majority were very close – within two miles.

## Question 4

a. 76
b. 25
c. 4

## Question 5

| | |
|---|---|
| Youth Club | 42 |
| College | 12 |
| Sports Club | 60 |
| Social Club | 58 |

## Question 6

80 men left school as early as possible.
17 spent one voluntary year at school.
8 spent at least two voluntary years at school.
63 men held CSE certificates
15 men held GCE certificates at 'O' level
3 men held GCE certificates at 'A' level
1 man held an Honours Degree

## Question 7

The most representative order was d, a, b, c, e

## Question 8

a 80; b 12; c 8; d 5

# Document C

Newshire Fire Authority,

Fire Brigade HQ,

Newstead Buildings,

Oldburn,

Newshire.

Dear Sir,

I am directed by the Chief Fire Officer to bring to your attention the vacancies which exist for retained men within the brigade and to invite you to apply for such a position. Fit, well disciplined men between the ages of 18 and 35 may apply in writing to the Chief Officer at the above address giving full details of their place and hours of work and stating their readiness to drill with the fire brigade on two evenings each week and to answer all fire calls to the best of their ability.

Applicants will be subjected to a medical examination and to an interview by Senior Fire Officers at which their suitability for work in the service will be investigated. It must be stated at the outset that personal ornamentation (rings, etc) and long hair will not be tolerated. A fireman's duty to his brigade and to the community comes before his duty to his family and the sacrifice of minor personal freedoms is part of the price he pays for the honour of serving others.

If you measure up to our high standards you will be welcomed among us and will find comrades for life.

Yours faithfully,

B Able
Station Officer

# Document D

Notes made during Meeting between Chief Officer and Administration Officer (Personnel)

Rates of Pay:   Retainer of £150 p.a.

             £10 per fire call

Uniform provided free of charge

Stress usefulness to employers of having trained firemen on premises. Firemen must be disciplined – long hair not acceptable because of risk involved.

Equipment – the most modern available. Drivers holding Heavy Goods Vehicles Licences especially welcome. Main reward of the job – saving others in their most dire need. Social facilities – snooker, darts and television provided at most Fire Stations. Convivial time in a local bar guaranteed at most stations on practice evenings.

Medical examination necessary, eyesight and hearing must be good. Training greatly improves most people's physical condition.

Stress the comradeship involved in belonging to a skilled, disciplined force engaged in work which is often hazardous. Many of our men have young families – perhaps such people recognise the importance of the fire service more than others.

Mention possibility of transfer to a full-time post – a rewarding career with every prospect of advancement to Fire Officer status.

Suggest interested men visit their local stations on practice evenings – number in phone book.

# Document E

**NEWSHIRE FIRE AUTHORITY**

**MEMORANDUM**

**From:**  Chief Officer

**Subject:**  Recruitment of Part-time Firemen

**To:**  Administration Officer
(Personnel)

**Date:**  10th March 198—

At a meeting of senior officers held last Thursday it was decided to offer a 'bounty' of £25 to any part-time firemen introducing another man to the force. The offer applies only to part-timers and is conditional upon the person introduced serving a minimum of 12 months in the Brigade. The bounty becomes payable after 12 months service by the person introduced.

An applicant should be introduced personally to his Station Officer by the part-time fireman concerned.

Prepare a notice to be sent to all Fire Stations for display on their notice boards setting out the offer clearly and the conditions attached. In addition write a covering letter to all Station Officers pointing out both the importance of the scheme to the Brigade's future and also that it remains the duty of all Fire Officers to search for suitable men as before, despite the fact that they, as officers, are not eligible for the bounty.

# Assignment 12 Assignment 12 Assignment 12

# *All Change*

You are one of seven clerical officers in the Estates Department of Messex County Council. Until now, your Department, which numbers eighteen full-time staff, has had inadequate accommodation in a former Junior School, at some distance from County Hall. The offices are draughty and dark, all cloakrooms and wc's are located in the basement and there are neither duplicating nor refreshment facilities, so the staff are constantly going backwards and forwards to the main building. There are no parking spaces in the vicinity and the public complain that not only do they have difficulty in finding the Estates Department but, because of the antiquated building, they have even greater difficulty in locating the person dealing with their query. A new extension to County Hall has recently been agreed, however, and your Department has been allocated the entire ground floor of this modern four-storey block.

In the neighbouring county of Farnshire, all the small Departments at County Hall are housed in open-plan offices. This type of office layout is being considered for the new Messex extension in the hope of cutting building costs. Your Head of Department favours the idea but would like more information since he needs to be assured that staff work efficiently and happily in such a setting. He therefore obtains Documents A and B (see overleaf) from Farnshire and asks you to prepare a report on the basis of these.

**Exercises**

1. Using Documents A and B produce a report for the benefit of your own Head of Department and other senior staff, outlining Farnshire staff attitudes towards working in an open-plan office. You are also asked to make recommendations, on the basis of the Farnshire experience, since some of their problems could then be avoided by Messex. (*Limit:* 400 words.)

2. Assume that, whatever the recommendations in your report, it has been decided to adopt open-plan offices for the new Messex extension and the architect and planner responsible have circulated diagrams, showing the *provisional* layout for the offices to all staff concerned in the move. The architect and planner have also agreed to talk over any complaints and suggestions from staff at a lunch-time meeting.

   (a) Prepare a notice to be placed in the Staff Canteen inviting all staff who will be moving into the new extension to a lunch-time meeting with the architect and planner. Try to impress upon them that it is to their advantage to go and give them some idea of the purpose and scope of the meeting.

   (b) Unfortunately, you will be away from Messex on the day of the meeting; but you would like your views to be known. Produce notes listing those of your present problems in the Junior School office accommodation

81

which will be remedied by the move to the open-plan office, any problems the proposed layout will not ease and any problems which might be *created* by the proposed layout. You intend to hand these notes to a colleague who has promised to put forward any of your points which are not raised by anyone else.

Base your notes on Document C (overleaf) which shows the proposed layout for *your* Department's office, and on the information about the Junior School accommodation which has already been given. (*Limit: 200 words.*)

(c) Using Document C for information and to allocate roles, conduct this meeting with Mr Wren (who favours the plan) as Chairman, and with the planner and architect present.

The planner and architect are worried by local Government cut-backs and by rising costs since a major hold-up at this stage, might affect the whole feasibility of the project.

3. Document D was distributed by your Head of Department in an attempt to ascertain the staff's colour-preference for the new office. While the result of this piece of office democracy does not seem in doubt, past experience has shown that your Head of Department, in fact, always follows his own inclination, without taking the general feeling into account.

You are asked to act for the Department by preparing a letter to your Head explaining the staff's determination *not* to have his colour choice in an office which is already poorly lit in parts.

The staff's views must be in writing, otherwise your Head can just ignore them – but since he is, at heart, more 'bumbling' than malicious, you must avoid hurting his feelings or creating too much tension.

You may sign your letter 'Staff Spokesman' so that no blame is attached to you personally. However, you are free to identify yourself if you consider that anonymity would be taken as a shield for tactlessness.

4. Prepare a questionnaire (for distribution to your Department, two months after the move) to find out if any problems have resulted from the move to the new office that might be put right.

Restrict yourself to ten questions or fewer.

# Document A

Results of a simple questionnaire distributed to Farnshire staff who are at present, in open-plan offices but who have also experienced convential office accommodation.

|  | Enjoy working in open-plan office | Do not mind what type of office | Dislike working in the open-plan office |
|---|---|---|---|
| *MALE* *Age 20–40* | *70%* | *20%* | *10%* |
| *40–65* | *54%* | *26%* | *20%* |

| | | | |
|---|---|---|---|
| *FEMALE* | | | |
| Age 20–40 | 60% | 35% | 5% |
| 40–60 | 59% | 21% | 20% |

# Document B

The questionnaire provided a section for 'comment' on the open-plan office and a cross-section of the opinions elicited is provided below:

Clerical
Staff

"you can gauge the flow of work better because you can see everyone . . ."
"It gives easy access to advice on difficult queries."
"I don't want everyone to know if I go and see the H.O.D."
"People are constantly walking about – I can't think."
"It's much more relaxed with all the grades mixed."
"I seem to be able to get through more work more efficiently."
"It's useful to have a 'relaxing area' nearby."
"It makes it very friendly; all being together."
"It's very noisy with no internal walls."

Secretarial
Staff

"I don't like the feeling of being looked at."
"The office feels so light and airy . . ."
"I've never spoken to our H.O.D. before . . . he seems a nice chap really . . ."
"We can take our queries straight to the person concerned by looking beforehand to see if he is busy with someone else."

Admin
Assistant

"I can actually see if someone is getting 'snowed under'."

Senior
Secretary

"Much more work can be handled. We have already caught up with our backlog from reorganisation and we are really on top of things. I think this is because internal communication has improved."

Deputy
H.O.D.

"The public do not have to wander from room to room trying to locate the person dealing with their application."

H.O.D.
(Head of Department)

"More team-spirit; certainly more efficiency."

Farnshire Questionnaire
December 1979

# Document C

OFFICE PLAN

100 feet long x 60 feet wide

Not to Scale

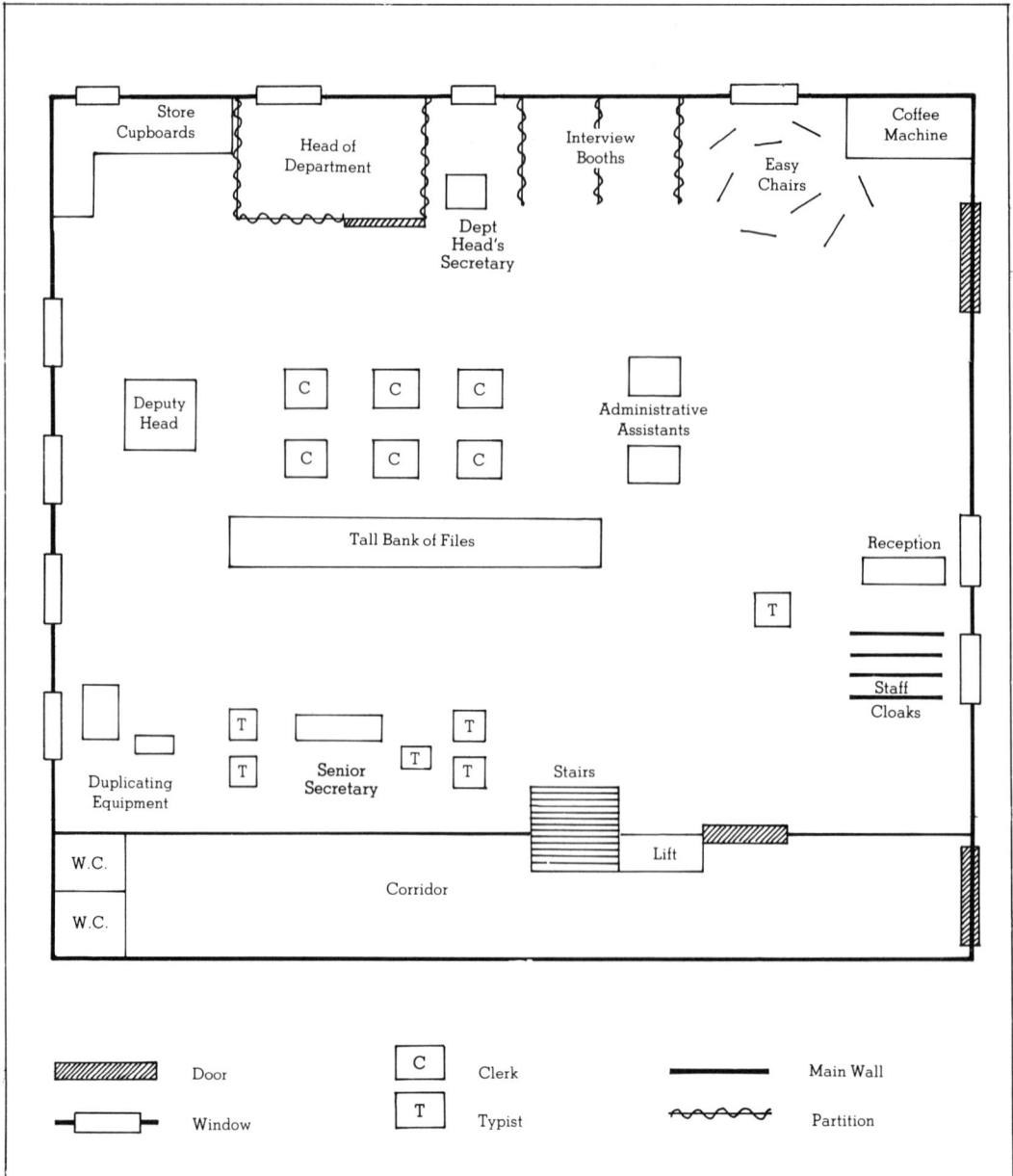

| | | |
|---|---|---|
| Store Cupboards | Head of Department | Interview Booths |
| | Dept Head's Secretary | Easy Chairs |
| Deputy Head | C C C | Administrative Assistants |
| | C C C | |
| Tall Bank of Files | | Reception |
| | T | |
| | T | Staff Cloaks |
| Duplicating Equipment | T T, Senior Secretary, T T | Stairs |
| W.C. | Corridor | Lift |
| W.C. | | |

Coffee Machine

**Legend:**

| Symbol | Description |
|---|---|
| ▨▨▨ | Door |
| ▭ (window symbol) | Window |
| C | Clerk |
| T | Typist |
| ▬▬▬ | Main Wall |
| ～～～ | Partition |

# Document D

To all staff,

I offer below the colour choices for our new office. I voted first and, as you can see, I prefer the royal blue and purple (rather dignified, don't you think?)

As it happens, I saw some military prints in a stationer's the other day which would tone in beautifully (mostly maroon and white). I managed to buy six at a reduced price and I would be most happy to donate them to the office.

M R WREN
Head of Department

### Colour Choices – Open-Plan Office

| | | |
|---|---|---|
| 1. | Royal blue walls, purple ceiling, light blue seating | Mr Wren |
| 2. | Wedgwood-green walls, white ceiling, olive seating | |
| 3. | Tan walls, mushroom ceiling, peat-brown seating | |
| 4. | Pale pink walls, rose ceiling, red seating | |

# Traffic Problems

You are employed by Winthrop County Council in its Roads and Bridges Department. Your Head of Department has given you a file containing Documents A to F and a set of instructions which are printed below. Follow these instructions carefully.

1. I want you to familiarise yourself with the traffic management scheme which we are proposing for Winthrop town centre by reading the enclosed documents. When you have done so, write a reply to the letter from the Chamber of Commerce (Document C) attempting to allay their fears. You will find the figures given in Document B very useful.

2. I am afraid that the general public is very suspicious of our proposals. Write a brief article, about 500 words will do, for inclusion in the *Winthrop Express*. Explain our reasons for proposing the scheme and answer the criticisms made in the "Express" last week (Document D).

3. We shall need to monitor public opinion very carefully during the next few weeks, so I should like you to draw up a brief questionnaire. Find out whether those questioned know anything about the scheme, what they think of it and why. You might bear in mind that you will be responsible for analysing the results – the more precise the answers are, the easier your job will be. Send the draft to the typing pool supervisor with a memo saying that I have authorised duplication of 2,000 copies; and tell her as tactfully as you can that we should like them this year!

4. We are by no means committed to this scheme yet, but we must do something soon. Take a fresh look at our proposals and tell me whether you really think we have got the right answer. As you can see from the Town Map, there are alternative routes we could choose. Write me a brief report saying whether or not you agree with our proposals and give me your reasons.

## Document A

Proposed Traffic Management Scheme for Winthrop

There is no traffic management scheme in operation at the moment and the bulk of traffic, whether local or passing through, uses the High Street. This causes considerable congestion, especially around the castle, and traffic frequently grinds to a halt during the summer months.

The Council proposes to divert Westbound traffic along Apple Lane, Brown Road and South Street, rejoining the High Street just beyond the main shopping area. Eastbound traffic will be diverted along Ford Road, Maple Road and Lucy Lane. The High Street and Keep Lane will be designated a traffic-free area, other than for delivery vehicles requiring access to the shops. Traffic lights will be set up at points A and B.

# Document B

Statistics Relating to the Use of Pedestrian Only Shopping Areas

| | Months since streets restricted to pedestrians | | | | | | | |
|------|-----|-----|-----|-----|-----|-----|-----|-----|
| City | 6 | 12 | 18 | 24 | 30 | 36 | 42 | 48 |
| A | 110 | 100 | 18 | 30 | 95 | 113 | 124 | 126 |
| B | 105 | 92 | 83 | 83 | 90 | 98 | 108 | 119 |
| C | 100 | 99 | 95 | 107 | 118 | 128 | 135 | 149 |
| D | 90 | 82 | 91 | 87 | 98 | 100 | 101 | 105 |

Figures expressed as percentages

100 = state of trade at time of opening as pedestrian areas

# Document C

Letter from Chamber of Commerce to the Clerk of the Council

Dear Sir,

I have been asked by my fellow members of the Winthrop Chamber of Commerce to inform you of our wholehearted opposition to your scheme for closing the High Street to traffic. It may have escaped your attention that practically the entire shopping area of Winthrop is located either on or adjacent to this street. The experience of sister organisations in other towns proves conculsively that we must expect a drop in trade of as much as 20% within twelve months of such a scheme being put into operation.

Shoppers are simply not prepared to walk from car parks to the shopping centre and as we already compete for trade with two 'conventional' shopping centres at Newtown and Oakley we fear that your proposals will drive many small shopkeepers out of business.

The effect of the proposed route on employment and general prosperity in Winthrop will be very marked and the Council will be held entirely responsible by those who suffer.

Yours faithfully,

R Sellers
Chairman, Winthrop Chamber of Commerce

# Document D

Selection of Comments by Local People Published in the "Winthrop Express"

1. The traffic may make the High Street unbearable at present, but at least leaves the residential areas undisturbed – this scheme would direct traffic to those very areas. Mr J Smith, Local Resident.

2. My school playing fields lie on the other side of Ford Road and I am very worried about the increase in traffic on that road envisaged by the Council scheme. Headmaster of Ford Road Secondary School.

3. Why don't the Council build a by-pass to the South of the town, that would solve everything? Mr R Atkinson.

4. Why should the townspeople have to suffer so that tourists can have a better view of the castle? We live here all year; they come for a couple of days at the most. Mr B Wilkins.

5. As Chairman of the Winthrop Historical Society, I would like to point out that all the buildings of historical and architectural interest are situated along the High Street. The fabric of these buildings has already suffered through exposure to heavy traffic and if the Council's scheme is not implemented soon we shall lose those buildings and the considerable tourist trade associated with them. The areas likely to be affected have no comparable historical interest and it should not be beyond the capacity of the Council to take the necessary steps to protect the inhabitants from traffic noise.

# Document E

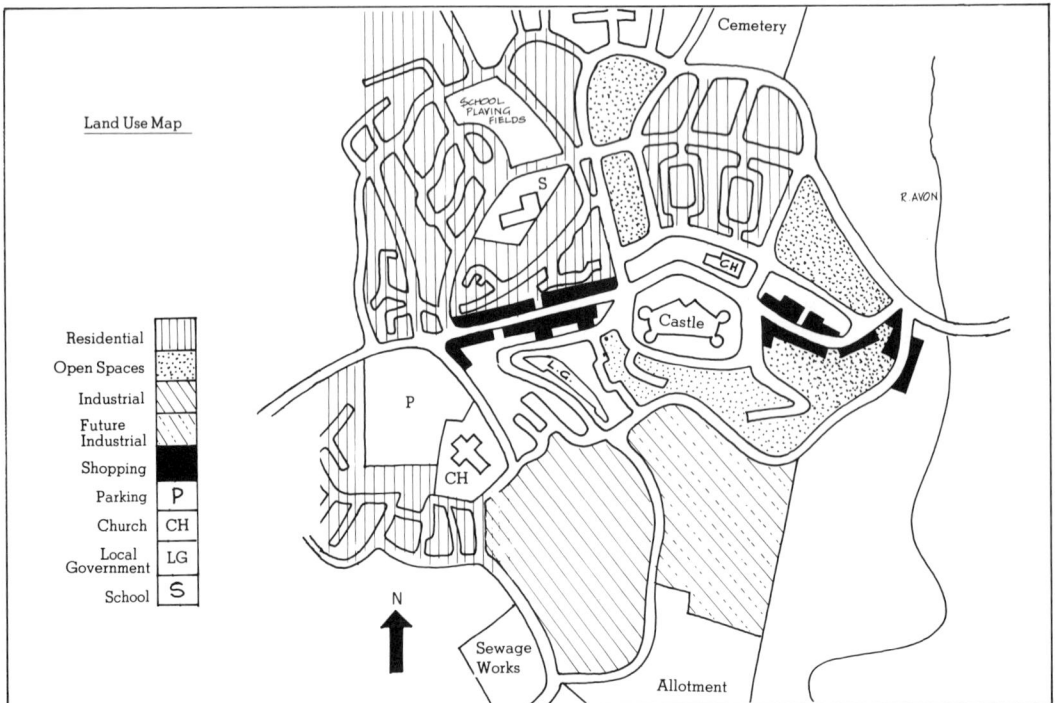

Land Use Map

| Residential | |
| Open Spaces | |
| Industrial | |
| Future Industrial | |
| Shopping | |
| Parking | P |
| Church | CH |
| Local Government | LG |
| School | S |

# Document F

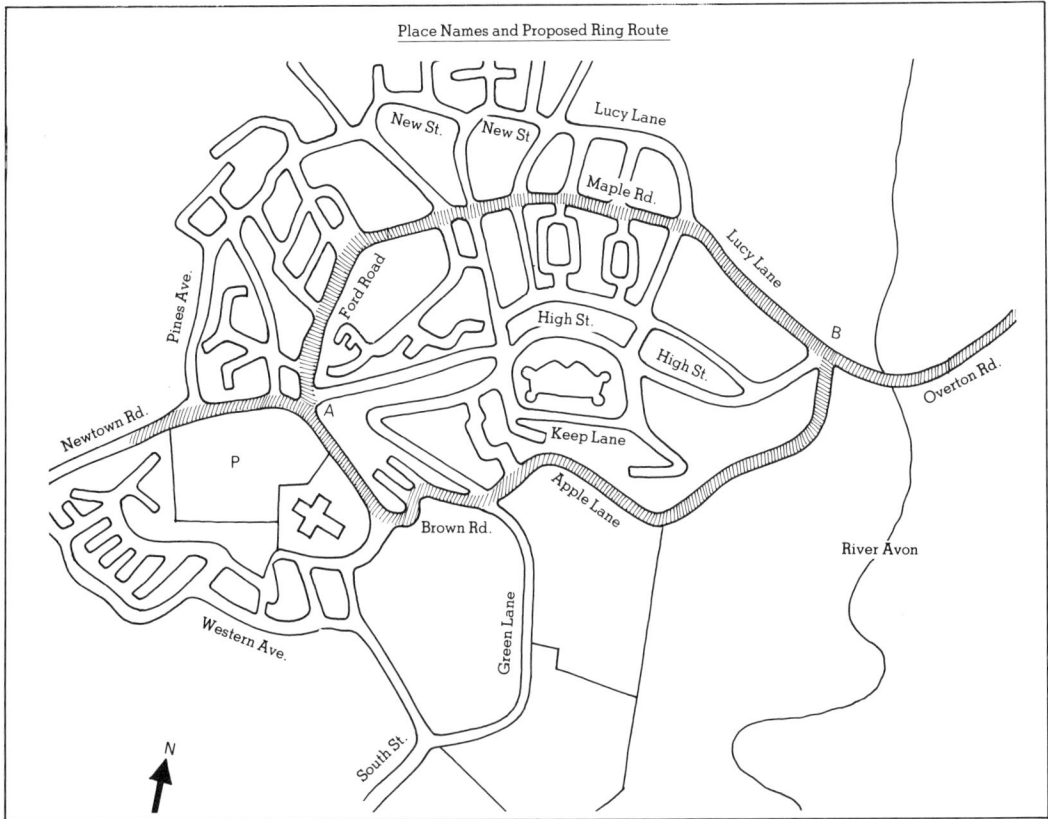

Place Names and Proposed Ring Route

# Oxton Finance Co Ltd

The picture represents the scene at the coffee break during a Board Meeting of Oxton's Finance Company. Oxton's is a family company employing 100 at their Head Office in Bexborough and having several small area offices specialising in personal credit facilities.

As a group, discuss the positionings in the picture and make suggestions as to the personality and relationships of those present by using body posture, dress and the Top Personnel Check List (given below) as your evidence.

## TOP PERSONNEL CHECK LIST (from left to right)

Mrs Stevens: Head of secretarial section. Now 40, has been with the firm since she was 16 and lives for her work. Not a Director but invited to be present for the discussion of business which she instigated.

Mr Greenshed: always worked in legal section of Oxton's, trained solicitor now a Director of the company.

Mr Davey: Director with responsibility for the day-to-day running of the Head Office. A distinguished war record, a personal friend of the Oxton family, age 60.

Mr Noam: Company Secretary, not a Director, been with the firm 15 years, now aged 46, both legal and accountancy training.

Mrs Hawley: 38, recently married, the grand-daughter of the company founder, a Director but with no specific role in the firm.

Mr Hawley: 40, worked his way up through the firm to become the Head of Finance but only on the Board since his marriage to the former Miss Oxton.

Miss Pritchard 34, newly-appointed personnel and training officer, not a Director, invited to the meeting to represent the interests of the staff in general.

In your own experience, what verbal and non-verbal signs might suggest:
1. Nervousness?
2. Irritation?

How do you think your own behaviour changes:
3. Under stress?
4. When you have been drinking alcohol?

(You may feel the need to mime the non-verbal signs or you could set up interviews to see how your class-mates do react under stress!)

# BOARD MEETING

*A transcript of part of the Board Meeting when the installation of telex – a proposition put forward by Mrs Stevens is discussed.*

| | |
|---|---|
| Mr Davey | Right, Mrs Stevens, if you could just fill us in on the background of this proposition . . . |
| Mr Greenshed | Legally speaking, I am not sure of how binding such a message would be – I think we'll have to check on that – but certainly, I can see that having something on paper will save time and money simply because a telephone conversation so often ends in a request for confirmation in writing. |
| Mr Noam | But this is my major worry, Mr Greenshed. Some of the communications made by this firm, particularly in matters of investment, require the greatest attention to detail and accuracy. At least, with a letter, it is checked at the time of signature so any error in transcription, on the part of a junior member of staff, can be spotted. |
| Mr Greenshed | But presumably this machine would not be available for use to junior members of staff at all . . . would it, Mrs Stevens? |
| Mr Davey | If it's at all complex my secretary won't be able to fathom it, anyway. She's a sweet young thing but not very mechanically-minded. |
| Mrs Stevens | In fact, anyone with typing experience would find it easy to operate once they are shown how, but, certainly, I had intended personally supervising its use, hopefully, finding |

|  |  |
|---|---|
|  | the extra time by delegating some of my less important ordering of stationery and stock-room work to my assistant, Miss Pagett, whose every spare minute is spent on the telephone, at the moment. |
| Mr Davey | Now see, we're creating more work for ourselves! |
| Mr Greenshed | Not necessarily, don't forget that as more and more firms become involved with telex, those outside the system become the odd men out . . . and, while Mrs Stevens has dealt with stocks and ordering very competently, I am sure her undoubted talents have not been stretched by this type of work and that a re-allocation of work-load might keep her junior staff on their toes (beams at Mrs Stevens). |
| Miss Pritchard | Certainly, the system was operated seemingly painlessly by my previous firm – although their having retail outlets did make it more important for them to be in daily contact over sales figures and stock position . . . |
| Mrs Hawley | Well, we have our branches, you know . . . (silence). When my grandfather started this firm there were just 20 employees. Now we have 100 at Head Office alone and ten offices along the South Coast with five or six full-timers in each, drumming up customers – never mind the part-time canvassing staff . . . (silence). We could send little messages to individual office Managers . . . keep them on the ball . . . increase our turn-over . . . that kind of thing . . . |
| Mr Davey | If only it were that easy, my dear lady . . . I remember, shortly after the war, when your father and I . . . |
| Mr Hawley | Oh Lord, just a minute, just a minute . . . You're thinking that every two-bit personal loan office will have one, aren't you? |
| Mrs Hawley | Well, yes. It's no use our having one if they haven't. Who else would we send messages to? |
| Mr Hawley | But these things cost £500 a time. Everyone can't have one can they? We'd be spending more a day in finding out how much we are making than we'd be taking in, in the first place! |
| Mrs Hawley | Oh, dear, sorry dear . . . . It's just that we used to be one big happy family. Daddy knew everybody by name and would pop to the area offices just for a chat. After all, the cheque trading side was the backbone of our business in the old days? |
| Mr Hawley | Well, it isn't now. Our main business is with other firms; with investment groups; with small companies who want capital for a particular venture and need our backing . . . . |
| Mr Greenshed | That's just why I feel we should move with the times. These types of people expect immediate replies – a modern attitude to business. |
| Mr Noam | In fact, Mrs Hawley, one of the benefits of this system is that the necessity for expensive pleasantries, so often indulged in over the telephone, for example, is removed. Messages become shorter, clearer and more business-like. |

| | |
|---|---|
| Mr Davey | Hang on, old chap. There's a limit, you know. There's still room for a double Scotch and a chat about the wife, I should hope . . . . |
| Mr Greenshed | Gentlemen, surely there is room for both attitudes here? No one could doubt the advantages brought to this firm by Mr Hawley's business acumen but, at the same time, we need not feel that by being up-to-date we will lose that personal touch of the respected family firm which has marked our dealings with clients. We will still have telephones, letters, even double Scotches...that's only civilised (waits for laughter) but what we will have, in addition, is a more efficient and economic form of business communication. |
| Mr Hawley | In the end, I do feel the decision should turn on money. If it is genuinely cheaper and I can be assured of no slip-ups, then I'm all for it. |
| Mr Greenshed | Perhaps the best solution would be for some disinterested party – possibly one selected by the Company Secretary – to quickly compile an analysis of telephone and telegram use within the office over a given day and compare it with the estimated cost in time and money if we had a telex machine. Then, since all other doubts appear to have been settled, the decision could be made totally on the basis of that report. |
| Mr Davey | Who will actually give the go-ahead, then, if it is necessary? We're not going to have to discuss it again, are we? |
| Mr Greenshed | Mr Noam, himself – if that would not be an inconvenience to him? (I do know how busy he is.) |
| Mr Noam | Well if . . . |
| Mr Hawley | That's OK by me as long as we all receive a copy of the report before Mr Noam takes any final action . . . Mr Noam? |
| Mr Noam | That should be no problem. |

**Exercises**

Using the transcript and any necessary reference works, answer the following questions and then compare your answers with the rest of the class.

1. What other advantages of telex are there, which are not mentioned?

2. How does a telex system operate?

3. Is a telex message legally binding?

4. What difficulties do you see in Mrs Stevens' personal supervision of the telex machine?

5. Who do you consider to be the least effective speaker and why?

6. (a)  Which speaker exercises the greatest unifying force in the discussion?

   (b)  What methods does this person use to hold a discussion together and what other methods are available?

7. What elements of Mr Hawley's reply to his wife reveal his irritation?

8. How might Mrs Stevens have presented her case better?

Using your own experience and judgment, answer the following questions and then compare your answers with the rest of the class.

9. Would you be pleased or worried if you were put in a position of authority?

10. (a) If you were in charge of a group of people, some of whom were older than yourself, some younger and some of the opposite sex, how would you exert your authority?

    (b) Would any part of this group present a particular problem to you?

    (c) Would your method of giving orders differ according to the sex or age of the person receiving the order?

11. (a) In a position of authority, would you take decisions which affect your staff (holiday rotas, the division of work, etc) democratically or autocratically?

    (b) What are the advantages and disadvantages of both systems?

12. Do you personally prefer to be told what to do or to be left to sort out your own work schedule?

13. (a) Within your class-group, which two people (you may include yourself) would you promote to be in authority over the rest? Why?

    (b) Which two people would you find most easy to work with? Why?

    (c) Which two people who seem to you to be intelligent or helpful or original, etc seem to be the least appreciated? Why? (You could avoid embarrassment by not naming the people and merely giving reasons – but praise never hurt anyone.)

# NON VERBAL COMMUNICATION

To demonstrate some aspects of non-verbal communication and the way that preconceived ideas about people affect our attitudes towards them, try the following game, which is used in some top level management courses in the USA.

**Exercises**     Separate into groups of 6-8 people (possibly with an observer who merely notes reactions). Without seeing what is written on their head-band, each person puts on a head-band and sits in a circle to discuss the best ways of getting staff to work harder. (Not a bad topic for discussion, whether you are playing this game or not.)

1. After about 10-15 minutes discussion, individuals should try and guess what role they were given by their head-band and they and the observer should report back to the main group on how their role affected their behaviour.

   The kind of roles given by the head-bands are:

   the boss     the whiz-kid     the boss's sexy secretary
   the half-wit son of the owner     the union boss
   the long-serving clerk, etc.

2. Also given on the head-band is some indication as to how everyone else should react to the wearer:

   eg the boss – respect and deference,
       the whiz-kid – praise every thought,
       the boss's secretary – chat up, but patronise,
       the half-wit son – be polite but ignore,

the union boss – treat with suspicion,
the long-serving clerk – to be walked over.

Obviously, it is more effective if the group do not know the possible roles beforehand and teaching staff could probably think of wickedly appropriate roles for specific groups by creating the head-bands themselves.

# NOTIFICATION AND ADVERTISING

You are employed by Oxton's the Finance Company, in their Head Office at Bexborough where there is a staff of 100. As a young and enthusiastic member of the Social Committee, you have been asked to help with the organisation of the firm's Annual Dinner. In previous years, the event has been held in early January at the Blue Boar (Document A shows prices and services offered). Usually, only 40 or 50 attend, mostly older or more senior staff and their wives. This year, the event should be more popular as some enthusiasm has been drummed up already, but you are hoping to gain the support of the younger staff (60% of the staff are under 35). You are now wondering whether a change of venue to the Bexborough Banqueting Rooms (Document B) might help to increase attendance.

**Exercises**    1 Using the information provided below, produce a report for the six members of the Social Committee, comparing the two possible venues with regard to entertainment, food, cost and any other factors relevant to their general suitability.

# Document A

---

### The Blue Boar
### Bexborough Road  Freesden
### Tel Freesden (063) 9311

**Seating for 100 in
the Banqueting Hall**
      
**Only four miles from
the city centre**

The Blue Boar is able to provide a wide choice of rather special wines.

Unfortunately, the floor is unsafe for dancing, but entertainment is provided by James Hearty and his Accordion Band.

#### Four-course Special Dinner for Parties

Choice of soups

Turkey/Beef/Veal or Pork with mixed vegetables

The Sweet Trolley

Cheeseboard and coffee             £5.00 inclusive of VAT
service extra

(20% reduction for parties of 30 or over)

---

2. Your recommendation having been accepted by the committee and your
booking having been confirmed for Saturday January 7th 8-12 p.m., you
must now advise all interested parties of the forthcoming event.

The five members of the Board of Directors are usually invited to the Annual
Dinner as the guests of the staff but the type of notification and advertisement
is left entirely to your discretion.

Make sample copies of all the communications you would produce for the
purpose of notification and advertisement.

3 Printed below is a copy of the speech which the Chairman of the Social
Committee was to deliver at the Annual Dinner. A domestic crisis means he
will not be able to attend, so you will have to deliver the speech for him. You
do not wish to simply read it out, so you decided to make notes on the speech
as an aid to memory.

Produce these notes, taking care that the layout allows for quick and easy
reference (and then deliver the speech to your group).

# The Chairman of the Social Committee's Speech.

Ladies and Gentlemen, it is my pleasant duty to welcome you here tonight on
behalf of your Social Committee. This gathering is certainly larger than any
other we have had and I hope that by the end of the evening you will be
convinced that the Annual Dinner is a date to look forward to.

Certainly, next year should be a particularly happy one for social activities, in
three respects: on the sporting side, I am pleased to announce that we can
now offer the staff subsidised squash and badminton facilities in the new
Bexborough Sports Club, every Tuesday evening. On the financial side, we
are happy to see that, despite this sporting innovation, funds are still fairly

healthy. Our normal sources of revenue, raffles and dances, have been very successful this last year, while the Car Treasure Hunt raised £30 in a highly enjoyable afternoon. Thus, the forthcoming year should see the installation of a dartboard and card-table in the staff coffee room; at long last. On the general activities side, we can affirm that the monthly social evenings can now be restarted. They will take place in the new Sports Club and, if we are to obey the architect, will be occasions for the baring of feet! Slippers or gym shoes are the only footwear allowed in the main hall of the Sports Club, but I do not suppose our fashion-conscious ladies will find much *comfort* in that thought (pause).

It is now my delightful duty to announce the winner of Oxton's 'Worker of the Year' contest. As you know, this is the first year that we have held such an event and it has proved to be most popular. Several candidates were proposed by the Section Heads, who had to give reasons for their choices, and then these candidates were short-listed by a committee made up of four Directors and Miss Pritchard. This short-list was then posted in the Staff Canteen two weeks ago and more than 50% of the staff exercised their right to vote. Miss Pritchard, the personnel officer, and her staff spent all last week counting these votes and in this sealed envelope I have the result of that ballot . . . . The name of the 'Worker of the Year' . . . wait for it . . . is Mr Peter Robinson . . . Head Caretaker, who I believe is sitting near the front on the right. Come on up Mr Robinson and collect your cheque for £20 and this charming cut glass vase, presented by Mr and Mrs Hawley. A round of applause, please, Ladies and Gentlemen for Mr Robinson . . . .

I am sure that this award is well-deserved since Mr Davey tells me that, over the past twelve months, you have halved the number of staff involved in cleaning tasks while maintaining the same high standard. I know this has meant some late nights and the ability to adapt to new ways and new machines but, as you can see, your employers and your work-mates are grateful for your efforts in the past and wish you the very best for the future . . . . Well done, Mr Robinson . . . another round of applause, Ladies and Gentlemen . . . .

Before I allow you to prepare yourselves for the delicious food, let me ask you to drink a toast to the Directors, who are seated on my left and who have provided the sherry to get the festivities started. Ladies and Gentlemen, . . . The Directors . . . .

On that intoxicating note, let me inform you that wine may be ordered through the waitresses and that the speed cops in Bexborough are pretty hot stuff! Seriously though, it looks as if the waitresses are ready, so, off we go, have a lovely time . . . .

*Notes*

*Notes*

*Notes*

*Notes*

*Notes*

*Notes*

*Notes*